GOD—THE ETERNAL PARADOX
and
OTHER SERMONS

GOD—THE ETERNAL PARADOX

and

OTHER SERMONS

ON THE PROPER GOSPELS
OF THE LENTEN SEASON

Edited by

PAUL ZELLER STRODACH

THE MUHLENBERG PRESS
PHILADELPHIA : PENNSYLVANIA

Made in the United States of America

Contents

iii

iv CONTENTS

CONTENTS

V

Foreword

COMMEMORATION of Our Lord's Passion and Death began in the earliest days of the Apostolic Church. The Season of Lent has developed from this early remembrance.

Preaching of the Passion began with Peter's Sermon on the Day of Pentecost, but with that was joined the preaching of the Triumph and the eternal Regnancy of the Risen Lord.

Augustine and Tertullian, two of the early Church Fathers, assert, that the Lenten Fast had its origin with the Apostles. But this is neither the Lent nor the Fast that we know; for both of these underwent a long process of development before they assumed the form and character familiar to us.

Their origin is probably to be found in the desire of the first Christians to perpetuate in the Infant Church the deep sorrow and mourning experienced during the hours of gloom and anguish when Our Lord was crucified and lay in the tomb. This period being just forty hours in duration gave some point to the length of time this Fast lasted; for it first appears as just forty *hours* long. But as that first sorrow gave place to the great joy in Our Lord's

Resurrection, so this Fast became quite naturally a period of devout preparation for the commemoration of His Triumph.

From this the idea of an *annual preparatory fast* developed. Quite early there is embedded in this a deep sense of what brought about the Lord's crucifixion, as well a reliving of the events which led up to it. It was not a far journey from this to a consciousness of individual sin and responsibility, and the consequent self-discipline and contrition.

One should never lose sight of the *natural* reasons back of these commemorations: the beginnings are such —loving memorials perpetuated by the early believers. Passing time adds many another touch; but when shorn of these, the origin remains an expression of adoring devotion, eloquent, sincerely purposeful.

Soon this brief period is extended: beginning with the Triumphal Entry it covers the entire week—the Great Week, the Holy Week. Then it grows to two weeks, beginning with the certain event in the Gospel wherein the outward enmity of the Jews is shown so markedly. (A remembrance of this still remains in the Church Year, Passion Sunday and the Proper Gospel of that Day.) This two-week period is the early *Passion Season*—today the Passiontide.

However, those who found so much in symbolism and mystical interpretation could not pass by the series of "Forcies": The Forty Hours, the Forty Days of Our Lord's Temptation in the Wilderness, etc. So the period of the Fast was lengthened to forty days and called the Quadragesima. The present custom of beginning Lent with Ash Wednesday is attributed to Gregory the Great: this period, excluding the Sundays (which are *in* but not *of* Lent), is exactly forty days in length.

It was a season of deep humiliation, of abstinence from social intercourse and pleasures. Fasting was practiced rigorously. Frequent and devout attendance at Divine Worship and the practices of private devotion were enjoined. Works of mercy and charity were to be performed. It was, and still should be, a season of deep penitence and mourning for one's sin. But for the Church it must ever be both a time of holy remembrance and a time to declare to the sin-sick world and the sin-sick soul the Grace of God in Christ Jesus, the Crucified and Ever-living Lord.

Of course there was "Lenten Preaching" through all these centuries: the voice of the Gospel of the Crucified and Risen Lord has never been still. But there is a difference between the Then and the Now. Lenten Preaching has attained to something of a distinctive character at this present day.

Perhaps this is the result of the influence of the Church Year (as much preaching in the liturgical Communions is certainly influenced by the various Days and Seasons in its course); but one is inclined to trace it to a somewhat different influence.

With the Reformation, preaching became a most strongly emphasized pastoral activity. Translation of the Holy Scriptures into the language of the Everyman of the day resulted in widespread, devout use. Men hungered for the Word, hungered to read it, hear it expounded—the pulpits resounded with the precious Gospel. It was honored and treasured as of priceless worth. And why? Simply because the Preaching of the Cross and Triumph of the Eternal Lord brought the healing of souls and the cleansing and strengthening of lives—Everyman was assured of the Grace of God in Christ Jesus, of finding and accepting it.

This period also produced many "helps" for personal devotion. Following the leads of the Medieval Church, the Evangelicals produced many little books of private prayer and devotion—Primers, "Paradises," Passionals, etc. It is not an overstatement, that the majority of these emphasized and centered in the Passion. No doubt the Passionals inspired the attempts to produce Harmonies of those sections of the Gospels which narrated the Passion and Crucifixion—the forefathers of the present History of the Passion. These were for both public and private use, and the Evangelical observance of Lent centered in both reading and preaching this History.

Lent became a season of devout remembrance, of

thankful, holy remembrance, of self-examination and cleansing, of uplifting of heart and life and spiritual nourishment, of prayer and adoration. The old "musts" were cleaned away: new *musts* appeared—"Woe is me, if I preach not the gospel"—"Hear, and your soul shall live!"

An *Evangelical* Lent inspired the Passionsandachten of the German and Scandinavian Churches and the Daily Services of the English. Where these were not possible, additional services on weekdays would be offered, and the Holy Week would bring a daily observance. All of these, whether daily or less frequent, carried the tone of the Holy Season, and this influenced both preaching and worship.

Our own observance of this season follows much in the line of such practice—a midweek service, perhaps an added one on Friday, throughout the period up to Holy Week; then daily services throughout that week. Some parishes have inaugurated a midday service during Holy Week and the Three-Hour Devotion on Good Friday in addition to the nightly ones. In some communities a daily noonday service has been instituted.

Now all of these services present opportunities for the declaration of the Word; and all of these start with an already provided "atmosphere"—but should it not be Theme or Ideal? This quite of itself will influence this round of preaching, and at the same time should inspire the *preacher* with a deep sense of his privilege and obligation. It is a rich preaching time!

One, *only* one, ambition should motivate him in his preaching—to witness to the Truth; to declare in all simplicity and selfless consecration the Word of the Cross and the Triumph of Faith, with whatever gifts of grace and understanding may be his. His message *in His Name* must ring true! If it comes from the conviction, love, and devotion in his own heart, it will. And part of this ambition will be to make good and careful preparation for the varied opportunities of preaching throughout this time. A devoutly thought out and well-ordered schedule is a prerequisite; and right here, all the riches of the Ageless Gospel are still at hand!

This will be the third year that a series of sermons based on the Gospels of the Lenten Season is issued. This year's series, like those which have preceded, are sermons which have been preached. They are the messages of the men who have delivered them, and they all ring true! Naturally they vary—certainly the men themselves do; and who would have them all alike? And no doubt, for such seems to be the natural or usual thing!—some will say of this or that sermon—"This one is good"—and of another, "This one is not so good!" But to all, we say— "They *all* are GOOD!"—for not one of them misses the Mark; not one of them has an uncertain voice; not one of them fails in witnessing. Here, too, the Apostolic word is true . . . "Having gifts differing" . . . they are waiting on their ministry faithfully.

PAUL ZELLER STRODACH

Septuagesima

GOD—THE ETERNAL PARADOX

PAUL SCHERER, D.D., LL.D., LITT.D., L.H.D.
Holy Trinity Church
NEW YORK, NEW YORK

The Proper Gospel for
SEPTUAGESIMA

For the kingdom of heaven is like unto a man that is an house-holder, which went out early in the morning to hire labourers into his vineyard. And when he had agreed with the labourers for a penny a day, he sent them into his vineyard. And he went out about the third hour, and saw others standing idle in the marketplace, and said unto them; Go ye also into the vineyard, and whatsoever is right I will give you. And they went their way. Again he went out about the sixth and ninth hour, and did likewise. And about the eleventh hour he went out, and found others standing idle, and saith unto them, Why stand ye here all the day idle? They say unto him, Because no man hath hired us. He saith unto them, Go ye also into the vineyard; and whatsoever is right, that shall ye receive. So when even was come, the lord of the vineyard saith unto his steward, Call the labourers, and give them their hire, beginning from the last unto the first. And when they came that were hired about the eleventh hour, they received every man a penny. But when the first came, they supposed that they should have received more; and they likewise received every man a penny. And when they had received it, they murmured against the goodman of the house, saying, These last have wrought but one hour, and thou hast made them equal unto us, which have borne the burden and heat of the day. But he answered one of them, and said, Friend, I do thee no wrong: didst not thou agree with me for a penny? Take that thine is, and go thy way: I will give unto this last, even as unto thee. Is it not lawful for me to do what I will with mine own? Is thine eye evil, because I am good? So the last shall be first, and the first last: for many be called, but few chosen.—MATTHEW 20: 1-16.

GOD—THE ETERNAL PARADOX

IN the twentieth chapter of St. Matthew, a householder is supposed to be speaking to a laborer who is disgruntled with his wages; and the householder says, "Friend, I do thee no wrong." Let's assume that the householder is God, which is what Jesus intends; and that He's speaking to you and me. Then it's clear at once how tremendously significant His words are. I have read them a thousand times. I think I *saw* them first quite recently! We might *remember* them the next time some so-called misfortune overtakes us; or when some huge calamity, as we think, lifts its head above the horizon and grows like a black cloud swallowing the sky.

Manifestly something has happened which to somebody looks like injustice. Some "wrong" has been done to somebody's way of thinking, and there are scowling faces and resentful eyes. When suddenly on the heels of it comes this gentle salutation: "Friend"! And all at once you understand that beyond the "wrong," whatever it is, there is no blind and stupid thoughtlessness, nor anything that could be regarded as just cruel chance; but a

3

quiet brow bent evenly and kindly on the life in front of
it: "Friend,—*I* do thee—no *wrong*."

I—So I suggest to you that we take it for God speaking; that against the background of our time we think
today of the even-handedness of the Eternal that does no
wrong, and the Love that keeps saying, "Friend."

You will remember no doubt the original setting.
Possibly we would better start by trying to picture it in
some more careful detail. Peter as usual had wanted to
know what he wasn't intended to know! He had asked
Jesus to say roughly how things would go with Matthew
there, and with James and John, and with himself. Now
that they had left their homes and the people they loved,
what could they expect in return? And he got this parable
for his pains!

At first glance it doesn't look quite right even to *us*.
A good *many* things do not. But put on your glasses and
examine it closely, and you'll begin to see how it was!
One day, said Jesus, there were some men who cannily
hired themselves out at six in the morning for a full day's
work; and they struck a tight bargain for a decent wage.
They weren't in business, as we say, for their health! And
what they had agreed *on* that they *got*, squarely at evening
time!

But they didn't like it! They didn't like it because
there were others who came to work in the vineyard at
nine and twelve; and *still* others who came as late as three

and five: and all these others received every man as much as *they* did when the day was done!

Now of course you couldn't complain about any lack of *justice* in that! So much is evident. The only thing you *could* complain about was the overdose of *generosity* doled out to the afternoon contingent; it never does strike us as particularly *fair* when somebody *else* who has done less to deserve it than *we* have gets as much of life's goods as *we* get! Although, if it's a matter of fairness, it must be remembered that here in the story these latecomers hadn't done any dickering with the lord of the vineyard! That's an important point. And it was rather decent of them. They had thrown themselves naked, so to speak, on the Master's bounty; so that if he wanted to *show* them some, it was really none of your business! At any rate, I think Peter got the point. It was a word to the wise! He'd have to *quit* asking such infantile *questions* as this: "What shall we *have* therefore?" Such questions just didn't *mean* anything with that kind of God around!

II—You see, therefore, that here as everywhere it's fundamentally the nature of God that concerns us. And that's always so. The secret of most of our difficulties with religion lies in our failure to realize what *kind* of God He *is*. Which is precisely why I'm making so much of it. We keep thinking, for instance, about God's justice. And the very shallowness of our thinking gets us into trouble. We talk of its being "tempered" with mercy. There's a common phrase for you; and the poison of a viper lurks in it. Little by little we begin to assume that at least where *we* are concerned God will water things down a bit. As nearly as we can make it out, He won't be quite accurate. He won't balance level those huge scales of His reckoning,— not like a jeweller, exact to a hairsbreadth: weighing out measure for measure, visiting, as He says, the iniquities of the fathers upon the children, three generations along and four. That's a bit overdrawn. He'll tip the beam with the finger of His compassion. He'll err a little on the side of long-suffering. He'll throw His love into it. He'll pile up the weight of His tenderness. Until what comes out in the end won't be justice at all. We're silly to lose any sleep over it. It will be justice "tempered" with mercy!

But that isn't what "tempered" means! To "temper" doesn't mean to "tamper"! That God will simply fool around with the idea in your case and mine, and doctor it up with no end of partiality and good will. Nor does "tempered" mean "diluted"! When you temper steel you make it hard and elastic, like a Damascus blade; you give it tone and vigor. There is a sense in which I'd be far less concerned about God's justice if He hadn't tempered it at all: it's His *mercy* that gives His justice its cutting edge!

I'm sorry we have lost most of the rigors of this thing out of our Christianity! Literature by itself should have kept them alive for us. The Greeks saw the dreadful inevitableness of what to them was Fate: how one wrong brought after it a *score* of wrongs, until men were no longer free at all, but were bound hand and foot by a kind of tragic necessity. Shakespeare saw it: as Macbeth and Hamlet and Othello one by one waded in so deep that "to turn back were as tedious as to go o'er!" Today we've come on the same dreadful inevitableness in human experience; a catastrophe vast enough to shame us forever out of our happy-go-lucky notions of the Judgment that sits undisturbed at the center of the world! With the kind of God a man can glimpse now, I'd hazard the guess, that life isn't a game He's playing for His own amusement, where the rules don't matter much!

But worse even than losing out of our religion the rigor of God's justice is this wild guess we make every time we think of this that we are God's *agents,* by whom He plans to deal at last with the Germans and the Japanese, to punish their treachery and their lust for power. We are caught with them in the common verdict which His holiness has pronounced against our kind of world! And there is something measureless and silent about it. Wars to end war are nonsense. And so are wars in defense of the Christian religion. We are fighting a war now to which the moral order of this universe condemns our blind and persistent immoralities. It's *worse* than *sin;* and it's *more* than *tragedy:* it's the *hell* for which our wilful life has been bent, and into which it has deliberately plunged at last with its eyes wide open!

If we make anything less of it than that, we're selling down the river of ruin generations yet to come. These puny little conversations we hear about inflicting grave penalties on whole nations when this madness is over are nothing but more madness. It's a kind of suicidal insanity to which great dignitaries of the Church of Jesus Christ are already affixing their solemn seal. There is to be a military occupation of Germany for a hundred years, and a partition of it into impotent principalities! If God is still God that's not the answer! It's nothing but a sharp weapon in Mr. Hitler's hands! Ultimately we're dealing with Somebody Who hasn't *reached* for power: He *has* it; and if there's vengeance, it's His! We'll instrument it at our peril. He doesn't care much about how we try to justify the attempt. The arguments we work up have very little weight with Him,—or with the laws of motion! History is His judgment; and on this one of its aspects it's absolutely ruthless!

I beg you therefore, against this tremendous canvas, for the sake of the future and your own soul, let's take out of our fatuous pictures, however big they are or little, what *we* want, and put into Life's sober pattern what *God* wants. That's as steady as it ever was. *We*'ve been inserting the *ifs* and *buts* and *althoughs; He* hasn't. And we are no longer in a position to go on with it: pick up this and lay down something else because we don't fancy it, and dismiss the whole thing on occasion. There are terrors in God's steadiness! I know that most of us don't want to hear about them. We mustn't be afraid. That's for the ignorant. Only ignorant people tremble. Let me tell you this: only fools don't! It was the gentle Jesus meek and mild Who said one day, My friends, *I* will forewarn you whom ye shall *fear:* not them that kill the *body;* but him who after he has killed has power to cast into hell. Verily I say unto you, Fear *him!* He knew what there *was* in God that couldn't be cajoled with an apple on His desk! Life isn't *like* that. It begins to look at the moment as if a little trembling were indicated!

III—But I want to come now to the other side of the picture. I want to indicate to you what is really the eternal paradox of God. A paradox isn't a contradiction. It's a double truth that can never be resolved into either one of its terms without the other. "Friend, I do thee no wrong." There's *justice* in it, and no less *justice* because of the *mercy* under those brows bent so evenly yet kindly on your soul. It's with the terrible justice of a God Who's in *love* with us that you and I have to deal! No watering down; but a tempering of His judgments until they cut like a surgeon's knife to heal! There is a Love that ranges this round, sad earth; and it searches and pursues and tears and exposes until our very souls are His!

To Isaiah God on one side is like a lion roaring, with his paw stretched out over Jerusalem as over his prey, never intending to give it up. And then in an instant on the other side He's like a mother-bird fluttering tenderly over her young, darting down now and then with her sharp beak at the glittering eyes of a snake. Studdert-Kennedy put the two sides together in his book of poems called "The Sorrows of God." There Christ to a cockney-soldier is a Presence full of "sweetness and rebuke," grim and gentle at once, which holds a man fast, staring, and has but a single word to say:

> "*All* eyes was in '*Is* eyes, *all* eyes,
>   My *wife's* and a million *more;*
> And once I thought as those two eyes
>   Were the eyes of the London whore.
>
>   .   .   .   .
>
> "There ain't no throne, and there ain't no book;
>   It's 'Im you've got to see,
> It's 'Im, just 'Im, that is the Judge
>   O' blokes like you and me.
> And boys, I'd sooner frizzle up
>   I' the fires of a burning 'ELL,
> Than stand and look into 'Is face
>   And 'ear 'Is voice say 'Well?' "

It's the love itself that cuts!

That's why there has always seemed to me to be such a tragic incongruity about the way in which we represent the figure of Justice. We put a sword in one of her hands and a pair of scales in the other: then we tie a bandage tightly over her eyes so that she can't see. We mean to say of course that she executes her judgments impartially; but with that bandage we say too much. We say too that she can't tell where to strike. And we say in addition that she can't read her own scales and never knows when they balance. Which is, ironically, precisely the trouble with *our* kind of justice. *God's* kind isn't blindfolded! It looks at you with the longing, faithful eyes of Jesus, and you can't turn them aside: they mean to win, with God's unbroken promise in them!

Strangely enough, the Jews learned that about Him for the first time during the very worst of all the years that ever overtook them: when in captivity they had nothing left; when the only future there was for them was the bitter memory of their great past, they were sure of it; when life had piled up its cruel odds beyond all reckoning. It was then and not before that they became conscious of a righteousness in God which was more than justice; a righteousness that meant the carrying through of all that He had ever said: against the temples and palaces of Babylon, with those magnificent winged-bulls that were only a trinket on the hem of her mighty vestments; against the tramp of armies and the sweep of empires. It was then and not before that they saw their own bleak History as His judgment; and straightway that became for them their best and sufficient reason for not giving up! For they saw too the *hope* that was in it because *He* was in it; and because He *was* what He *was*. These snow-capped mountain peaks of the Old Testament rise out of that experience, as the majestic summits of the Alps rise out of the clouds

that brood darkly over the valleys. It's the love that's in
His justice which cuts through to the human soul—then
gives it ground for its feet and an air to breathe, as it lifts
its head, like the air of the morning!

I wonder if it can't make *us* steadier too? It's the kind
of God we come on at the cross. He isn't defeated. He's
just seeing it through! Jesus was never pushed about
and pressed into a corner and nailed fast. Nobody in Jerusalem that day was as quiet and uncompelled as He. Pilate
went in and out wringing his hands; but never once was
Christ twining and untwining His fingers as if He didn't
know what to do. So it's *we* who are helpless now, *not*
God. *He* has in His grip—*we* don't!—these days and
these years, and what we've done to one another and to
Him! They are the most damning judgment Life has ever
written against itself; but with the very sound of the hammer on the nails there comes pressing in again upon the
world this utmost, most overwhelming concern, which
broke once the heart of God! It's not the concern any
longer of a limp and lifeless Figure on a cross, but of One
Who is stalwart now with the centuries. His head isn't
drooping any more. His face looks straight on. It's a poor
pass to which His Love has been brought again; but with
their regal calm His eyes leave the issue out of all doubt!

If only you could *see* Him there, whatever it is that
has taken place in your own soul or in the world and hear
Him whispering, "Friend, *I* do thee—no *wrong!*"

Sexagesima

"HE THAT HATH EARS..."

EDWARD T. HORN, III

Lutheran University Pastor
Cornell University
ITHACA, NEW YORK

The Proper Gospel for

SEXAGESIMA

And when much people were gathered together, and were come to him out of every city, he spake by a parable: A sower went out to sow his seed: and as he sowed, some fell by the way side; and it was trodden down, and the fowls of the air devoured it. And some fell upon a rock; and as soon as it was sprung up, it withered away, because it lacked moisture. And some fell among thorns; and the thorns sprang up with it, and choked it. And other fell on good ground, and sprang up, and bare fruit an hundredfold. And when he had said these things, he cried, He that hath ears to hear, let him hear. And his disciples asked him, saying, What might this parable be? And he said, Unto you it is given to know the mysteries of the kingdom of God: but to others in parables; that seeing they might not see, and hearing they might not understand. Now the parable is this: The seed is the word of God. Those by the way side are they that hear; then cometh the devil, and taketh away the word out of their hearts, lest they should believe and be saved. They on the rock are they, which, when they hear, receive the word with joy; and these have no root, which for a while believe, and in time of temptation fall away. And that which fell among thorns are they, which, when they have heard, go forth, and are choked with cares and riches and pleasures of this life, and bring no fruit to perfection. But that on the good ground are they, which in an honest and good heart, having heard the word, keep it, and bring forth fruit with patience.—LUKE 8: 4-15.

"HE THAT HATH EARS..."

ONE of the great arts which has all but disappeared in these days of ours is the art of intelligent listening. We all want to talk at once and without end. We pride ourselves on being good conversationalists. We speak the praise of the man in whose presence conversation never lags. Our mail boxes are filled with printed and duplicated words. Everybody wants to write a book. Our radios talk at us incessantly from dawn until midnight, yet we seldom pay attention unless there is a thirty-seconds' pause. Then we are sure that the transmitter has broken down, and the announcer apologizes profusely for the half-minute of silence. We are often like the anonymous lady who attended a concert given by a famous symphony orchestra, and complained afterwards that the intermission was far too short. "They should," she said, "have allowed us an extra fifteen minutes. I didn't get to talk to half my friends."

As we read the Gospel for Sexagesima Sunday, we can almost imagine that the many people who had "come to him out of every city" did not listen too attentively to

15

Jesus, either. For when he had finished, we are told that "he cried," and the Greek word means "spake with a loud voice," as though it may have been necessary for Him to regain their wandering attention. Some scholars have believed that this was the first occasion upon which Jesus used the parabolic method of teaching, and some of His hearers may have been saying to themselves (if not, indeed, to their neighbors), "Here we came ten miles to hear Him speak something profound, and all He does is tell us a story of a man going out to sow a field!"

Poor listeners! They did not recognize in the homely figure of the sower, Him that spoke; or in the seed, God's Word; or in the rustic tale the foreshadowing of His own eventful life; or even in the sun-baked wayside, the rocky subsoil, or the thistled patch, themselves!

And had they realized the full import of His words, being men of human nature like ours, they would have forthwith blamed the sower and the seed. In our day this is a favorite pastime. A modern critic writes, "I cannot help wondering, too, whether the religion which the church gives us is not, on the whole, rather less interesting than it used to be. . . . I have the general impression that the brains of the country are not trooping into the pulpit."[1]

---

[1] Pratt, James Bissett, Professor at Williams College, in "Religion and the Younger Generation," an article in "Contemporary Thought," edited by Kendall B. Taft, John Francis McDermott, and Dana O. Jensen; published by Houghton Mifflin Company, 1929. The reference is to page 343.

To be sure, clergymen have their faults. But despite the fact that they may not be perfect sowers because of shortcomings common to all human nature, the Word is being spread broadcast today in more fields than ever before in history. And among the sowers are and have been men of Christlike piety and devotion who have suffered the keen disappointment of seeing the seed wasted on barren ground. Like their Master, they have led; too few have followed.

If the sower is not at fault, we say to ourselves, then the fault must lie with the seed. It does not germinate as it should. The Word has, in these latter days, lost its power. And immediately we find ample support among the critics of Christianity. We are told that the authority of the Word is gone forever; that the new gospel is a Utopian humanism; that the new Bible is the word of science; that religion perished on the same day with its twin—superstition. Against this stands the Word itself. "Heaven and earth shall pass away, but my words shall not pass away." So spoke Jesus, and twenty centuries of Christian experience bear out in retrospect the truth of His statement. In every Christian generation, there are and always have been those "which in good and honest heart, having heard the word, keep it, and bring forth fruit with patience." Their host rises up to confound us when we try to make a case for the sterility of the seed.

For the truth is that the sowers may be men of Christian piety and godly love; the seed may be the pure Word of God; and yet the quality of the harvest—in fact, whether there is to be any harvest at all—depends upon the soil. What matters is the receptiveness of the hearer, and his ability to translate what he hears into effective and constant Christian growth.

It is not easy to listen well. Even the Church itself has not always properly attuned its ear to God's Word. At times it has been impervious; at times shallow; at times "choked with the cares and riches and pleasures of this life." At times it has been so engrossed in activism that it has not had time to listen. At times it has tried to become so modern that it has cut itself off from God's Word as it has been revealed to the hearts and minds of godly men of other times. At times it has even mistaken the voices of men for the voice of God.

But amid all these mistakes, there have always been some who have listened and have heard. The prophets listened to God's Word. They could then go forth and condemn kings with a word which was not their own. The psalmists meditated, and out of their quiet contemplation came their hymns of praise. Jesus withdrew alone, and out of that solitary communion with His Father came the power that astounded the world. Paul heard God's voice in mystical experiences and went out from them armed with His Word. And an eminent modern philosopher, Professor William Ernest Hocking, head of the Department of Philosophy at Harvard University, suggests[2] that the power of the Renaissance and the Reformation may have been derived from the great reservoir accumulated by medieval piety through ages of contemplation! Certainly the power latent in him who listens to God has been and is vastly underestimated.

But how shall we listen? Our thought forms and mind sets are occidental, not oriental. The experiences of Jesus are in a class by themselves, although we can learn much from them. But we are not given to mysticism and ecstatic experiences as were the prophets, the psalmists, and Paul. Nor are we of a piece with Erigena, Bernard of Clairvaux, Meister Eckhardt or the other mystics of the middle ages. This is an age of speed and action and we are, or at least like to think we are, matter-of-fact realists and activists.

Fortunately, we do not need to be mystics to hear God's Word. We have, for one thing, a more complete and accurate Scripture than they had, and God speaks to us from every page if only we will read. There is no substitute for the Bible. A man might just as well expect to be a research chemist without ever having studied the table of elements, as expect to be a Christian without studying Christianity's source-book. One of the most pathetic sights is that of a group of college young people

---

[2] Hocking, William Ernest, Professor at Harvard University, "What Man Can Make of Man," *Fortune*, February, 1942, page 136.

trying to find the correct application of Christian principles to a modern social problem, without any knowledge
of the basis of the Christian principles involved—solely
because they are Biblically illiterate! The Bible—the book
that should be the most thumbmarked of any book in any
Christian home—how often it is dusted off and set out on
a conspicuous table only when the minister is coming to
call! The seed hid in a closet! No wonder there is no
harvest in the field!

And we have, for another thing, God's Word in the
services of the Church. It is remarkable to what strange
lengths some people will go to try to find His Word anywhere but in His House! His Word has been sought and
allegedly found along the bridle path, in fields and woods,
in brooks and waterfalls, in the wild fury of the storm,
and the quiet glory of an evening sunset. To be sure there
are evidences of God in nature, but it is the deist's god.
To find the God and Father of our Lord Jesus Christ, and
to hear what He has to say to us, we visit His House. Visit
it alone sometime, and worship by yourself, although we
Protestants have made that difficult by locking our
churches during the week as though God could speak only
on Sunday mornings!

But visit it, too, with me on Sunday morning. The
week has been hard. The world is in a turmoil. My plans
and yours are all upset because of it. We, and millions like

us, are confused by the babble of many voices rising in a great crescendo.

"I sought relief within the quiet church
From earthly tumult, clamor, strife and din;
Silent the massive doors behind me shut
The world without—God's Word and me within."

Before The Service starts, His Word is there. The tall candles, lit upon the retable, speak of Him Who is His Word and Who is the Light of the world. The crucifix upon the altar speaks of Him Who died for our sins; and, imagining the corpus removed, the empty cross speaks of Him Who rose again and through Whom we have eternal life.

The organ plays. This is not worldly music, but the majestic music of a master three centuries dead, through whose fingers and keyboard the Word spoke. The hymn begins. It is not religious ragtime, but stately melody pouring out the soul of one who felt the presence of the Word and was moved to sing it forth.

The minister stands before the entrance of the chancel in silent prayer. He is not clad in the business dress of the world, but in the historic vestments of the proclaimers of the Word. He speaks and the Liturgy begins, but the words he speaks are not his own—they are God's Word.

We ask forgiveness of our sins, and are assured with God's Word that we have been forgiven. The Introit from the choir proclaims from God's Word the theme for the day. We sing that ancient Christian hymn, *Gloria in excelsis Deo,* and I hear angels singing God's Word over the fields of Bethlehem long ago.

We pray a Collect—not one suiting the minister's own whims, but one fit to this very service, composed perhaps in some monastery a thousand years ago by a holy man long since become unknown, whose prayer inspired by God's Word, lives on forever!

God's Word is in the Epistle for the Day; the choir sings it in the Gradual; and then we rise to hear the Word of Words—the Gospel. We confess our faith in the words of the Nicene Creed. The words are not ours, but in phrases penned by men inspired by God's Word, they show forth what the Church has always believed and always will believe.

Another hymn, in harmony with the Lessons for the Day and foreshowing the Sermon that is to follow. And then the Sermon. The minister is not the most eloquent speaker in the Church. But he speaks with earnestness and from the heart. He does not "put on a show" in the pulpit, or use sensational subjects to draw listeners to his church. He does not speak of world events, of economic problems, of social maladjustments as such. Instead, he preaches on a subject that belongs to God's Word for this very Sunday. For he knows in all humility that he is only the voice through which God speaks to His people His Word.

Some ancient psalmist penned God's Word in the Offertory. The General Prayer—not in the minister's words, but in stately, churchly phrases—asks that in all the vicissitudes of human existence, God's Word may dwell among us.

Another hymn speaks from God's Word of preparation for the joyful reception of His Sacrament. The Preface and the *Sanctus* tell of the agelessness of the Word. The Lord's Prayer brings the Words of Christ Himself; the Words of Institution are quoted from Scripture; the prayerful litany, *Agnus Dei*, recalls His Word and what it has meant to the countless Christians who have repeated it in many centuries at communion.

We go to the altar, kneel, and hear His Word as we eat the wafer with which His Body comes to us. We hear His Word as we drink from the chalice the wine with which His Blood comes to us. We hear the eucharistic benediction, we rise and return to our places to pray. The communion vessels are veiled and we sing God's Word as it fell from the lips of Simeon in the beautiful *Nunc Dimittis*. Our thanksgiving continues in psalmody and prayer; and the Benediction with which, since Moses' day, God's people have gone forth, is pronounced upon our bowed heads. In silent prayer we ask that God may grant us grace to carry forth from this place His Word into the world that we may be better men and earth may be a better place.

"I left the quiet church and started forth
  To face the toil and bustle of the day.
The strife without I did not hear within
  Where God's Word said to me, 'I am the Way'."

On this Sunday, the Church looks forward to Lent. The events which are perennially recalled then are fraught with deepest meaning. The Word that became flesh amid such joy on Christmas Day is about to be shuffled off to Calvary by men like us. What does it mean for us? Who but God can tell us? And beyond the gloom of the Cross, there is the glorious sunburst of an Easter dawn—and an Empty Tomb. What does it mean for us? Who but God can tell us?

"He that hath ears to hear, let him hear."

Quinquagesima

GOING TO JERUSALEM

J. HAROLD MUMPER, D.D.
Keller Memorial Church
WASHINGTON, DISTRICT OF COLUMBIA

The Proper Gospel for

QUINQUAGESIMA

Then he took unto him the twelve, and said unto them, Behold, we go up to Jerusalem, and all things that are written by the prophets concerning the Son of man shall be accomplished. For he shall be delivered unto the Gentiles, and shall be mocked, and spitefully entreated, and spitted on: and they shall scourge him, and put him to death: and the third day he shall rise again. And they understood none of these things: and this saying was hid from them, neither knew they the things which were spoken. And it came to pass, that as he was come nigh unto Jericho, a certain blind man sat by the way side begging: and hearing the multitude pass by, he asked what it meant. And they told him, that Jesus of Nazareth passeth by. And he cried, saying, Jesus, thou son of David, have mercy on me. And they which went before rebuked him, that he should hold his peace: but he cried so much the more, Thou son of David, have mercy on me. And Jesus stood, and commanded him to be brought unto him: and when he was come near, he asked him, saying, What wilt thou that I shall do unto thee? And he said, Lord, that I may receive my sight. And Jesus said unto him, Receive thy sight: thy faith hath saved thee. And immediately he received his sight, and followed him, glorifying God: and all the people, when they saw it, gave praise unto God.—LUKE 18: 31-43.

GOING TO JERUSALEM

TODAY we have come to the last Sunday before the beginning of the Lenten season (Quinquagesima)—that season during which we spend much time in the contemplation of our Lord's suffering and death. But at the same time—and never let us forget this—it is the season which shall end again in our Lord's glorious triumph over death, and His return to life for evermore.

It seems most appropriate, then, that our meditation shall be based upon the appointed Gospel Lesson for today, which is Luke's account of the announcement Jesus made of His intention to go up to Jerusalem, there to begin this very season which we know now as Lent.

Our text is the very simple statement of Jesus to the disciples just before that journey began:—"Behold, we go up to Jerusalem, and all things that are written by the prophets concerning the Son of man shall be accomplished" (Luke 18: 31).

The first thing that impresses us at this time in Jesus' life, is His loneliness. Now we don't mean for a moment that Jesus was alone physically. As a matter of fact, quite

the opposite was true. He was at this very moment sur-
rounded by His disciples. And whenever He made a public appearance, He was always in the midst of a multitude.
But one can be terribly alone in a multitude as some of us
very well know. It is one of the worst forms of loneliness
possible. But this loneliness of Jesus was different even
from that. His was the loneliness of ideals and purposes
and knowledge which were far beyond the comprehension
of those who were His most intimate friends.

Contrast, if you will, His ideals with those of the two
brothers, James and John. Jesus came into His life work
for the sole purpose of establishing the true Kingdom of
God on earth—a kingdom not temporal in any sense, but
rather a spiritual kingdom, based upon brotherhood and
love and mutual esteem and service and self-sacrifice. He
came to reveal God to men and to set the example to all
men to become Godlike. But just at this point in His life,
these two brothers, James and John, came to Him. Mark
says they came in person, the other Synoptists say that they
sent their mother to ask, that when Jesus came into His
Kingdom, they, James and John, should be granted the
privilege of sitting, the one on His right hand and the
other on His left. You see, their conception of the Kingdom of God was a purely earthly one. Even at this point,
after three years with Jesus as disciples, they still clung
to the common Jewish conception of the Kingdom, namely
that it was to be the re-establishment of Jewish rule, under

a descendant of the great King David, and they wanted to be secretary of state and keeper of the privy seal, respectively.

You see, Jesus ideology had not yet gripped them. His high and holy purposes were not yet theirs. Even the relation—the specific relation in detail of the events that would take place at Jerusalem went completely over their heads. They missed the point entirely. Luke says, in the thirty-fourth verse of this eighteenth chapter, "They understood none of these things."

It is not surprising, then, that the knowledge of that fact led Jesus to know that He was standing alone, and would have to stand alone until His sufferings would be past and the realization of what had happened would gradually dawn on His disciples.

But many of those who have done most to benefit mankind have had to stand alone:—Jesus in Gethsemane, Martin Luther before the Imperial Diet at Worms, Columbus before Ferdinand and Isabella, Washington in the snows at Valley Forge, Lincoln kneeling in the White House, Doctors Curie toiling in the muck to discover the life-giving particles of radium—all have been lonely figures.

Nor will you find it an uncommon lot today. Those of us who are trying to maintain in our own lives, and to set forth before others, the high ideals and the definite instruction of Jesus, will not find ourselves the center of a cheering multitude, but often very much alone and, not infrequently, misunderstood and even persecuted by those who have permitted other ideologies to "black out" the real aims and purposes of the Christian faith.

But then comes most certainly the second thing that impresses us as our Lord starts His journey to Jerusalem. It is His indomitable courage. He knew what He was facing. Listen to His words again as Luke records them:— "For he (the Son of Man) shall be delivered unto the Gentiles, and shall be mocked, and spitefully entreated, and spitted on: and they shall scourge him and put him to death" (Luke 18: 32, 33). He knew that. But still He set His face steadfastly to go to Jerusalem. Why? Simply because He knew that He would have to stem the tide of opposition at its source. He would have to purify the spring where it arose. He would have to teach His truths, preach His Gospel, live His matchless life in the nation's capital, at the very heart of the nation's religious and cultural life. And He knew that the opposition there was such that that procedure would spell out His death and nothing else. But He also knew that His death would accomplish what nothing else could. Sometimes it does take blood to correct the evils of the world and to set men to thinking straight concerning the affairs of this life. So with high, inspiring courage, our Lord went to Jerusalem, knowing full well what would befall Him there.

Today we are faced with a series of situations which

call for that type of courage. Forces of evil are released throughout the world that threaten to engulf and destroy all the agencies for good that there are in the world. In times like these, it is easy to point fingers, call names, hold courts of inquiry to fix blame, and do a thousand and one other things which not only build up hatred for an enemy, but which also tend to divide the sentiments, and, consequently, the force of a people who should be united now as never before. Today the safety of the world is seriously threatened; not only the physical safety, but much more the moral safety. For war not only jeopardizes the physical wellbeing of people, but it tends to declare a moratorium on the ordinary morals of people—to say nothing of a moratorium on Christian ethics.

So this situation, too, calls for a display of courage— the kind of courage that Jesus displayed as He set His face steadfastly to go to Jerusalem, knowing that He would die there, but knowing also that that very death would accomplish God's high and holy purpose.

Now we're not afraid of the American people when it comes to a display of physical courage. We are noted for it. But what we need even more than we need physical courage is moral and spiritual courage—courage that will dare to speak and live for God while the war is on and when the war is over. If we permit the ideals of Jesus to lapse just because there is a war on; if we lose sight of the ideals of love and brotherhood for all mankind, just be-

cause we were attacked by enemies into whose hands we
ourselves placed the weapons for that attack; if we condemn our enemies as godless heathen, when we ourselves
have never been very seriously concerned about making
them Christian brethren; and if we, at the end of the conflict, demand the last Shylock's pound of flesh, then every
drop of blood shed and every dollar spent either advisedly
or wastefully will have been spent in vain. If, on the other
hand, we realize the grimness of the situation, but go forward unitedly to do this distasteful thing that has to be
done—but do it with "malice toward none and with
charity for all," accepting the fact that the guilt is partly
ours, and determined that our relations with other countries in the future will be different and, if possible as much
as lieth in us, Christian, then the results will be worth all
it cost—even as the result of Jesus' death is worth all the
price He had to pay on Calvary.

But the choice again is ours, and what we need now,
probably more than anything else, is the courage to carry
on our moral and spiritual program on a high plane, even
in the midst of opposition and criticism, and perhaps even
a natural tendency to do otherwise.

The third thing that impresses us as we begin this
journey to Jerusalem with Jesus, is the fact that He didn't
permit concern about Himself to interfere with His
thoughtfulness of others. One would naturally suppose
that if a man were going to die within the next week or

so, and knew it, He could think of little else, and would do everything possible to avoid it. But, instead, Jesus went right to the place where His enemies held power, and on the way there He stopped to minister to the needy along the way, as in the case of the blind man at Jericho.

The rationing of commodities in wartime has revealed a lot of things and a lot of characters. At the beginning of the rationing, a man was boasting about his own smartness with relation to this business. He boasted about how he saw this coming, and how he immediately bought complete sets of tires for all *three* of his cars and laid in a couple hundred pounds of sugar. Well, that is just the kind of spirit that has brought on this world condition in which we are now. Just multiply that man's spirit and action to national proportions, and you have greedy nationalism which looks out for the capital "I" with utter disregard for one's neighbor and his needs. "What do I care if my neighbor has not my foresight or my means? *I* have them, and I'll look out for *ME*—let the other fellow be rationed, even starved! It won't affect ME, for, you see, I'm SMART!"

Nothing could be farther from the Christ spirit than that. Yes, these times are revealing times. We once heard an army officer say that the battle line does not make either cowards or heroes, it only reveals them. They were actually made long before they reached the battle line. Jesus, facing the greatest ordeal of His life, at a time when one would think that He could think of nothing but Himself and His own impending death, nevertheless had time to turn aside and minister to those in need. What a lesson for us, in these days!

Now finally, we are impressed by another thing about Jesus as He set His face toward Jerusalem, and that is His confidence. You will note again how specific He was about His sufferings and death, but you will note also that He was just as specific about the ultimate outcome—"And the third day he (the Son of Man) shall rise again." And He felt that that final outcome would be worth all that it would cost—and it was. May we revert to something we said just above? If, out of these present world conditions, these sacrifices, these privations, there shall come sight for the world—a realization that Jesus was right when He declared, "I am *the* way!"—the only way to peace and contentment and universal understanding; if out of all this chaos there shall come a readjustment so that the principles of freedom shall be put into practice—then the outcomes of these bitter experiences shall be worth all they cost. We must rededicate our lives to that end.

Ash Wednesday

KEEPING LENT

JOHN W. RILLING, S.T.M.
First Church
SPRINGFIELD, OHIO

The Proper Gospel for

ASH WEDNESDAY

Moreover when ye fast, be not, as the hypocrites, of a sad countenance: for they disfigure their faces, that they may appear unto men to fast. Verily I say unto you, They have their reward. But thou, when thou fastest, anoint thine head, and wash thy face; that thou appear not unto men to fast, but unto thy Father which is in secret: and thy Father, which seeth in secret, shall reward thee openly. Lay not up for yourselves treasures upon earth, where moth and rust doth corrupt, and where thieves break through and steal: but lay up for yourselves treasures in heaven, where neither moth nor rust doth corrupt, and where thieves do not break through nor steal: for where your treasure is, there will your heart be also.—MATTHEW 6: 16-21.

KEEPING LENT

THE powers of evil have won their greatest triumphs by capturing the organizations which were formed to defeat them, and history seems to show that when the devil has thus changed the contents of the bottles, he never alters the labels. The fort may have been captured by the enemy, but it still flies the flag of the defenders." So writes Dean Inge. The truth of this sober judgment is verified, as nowhere else, by the events that led up to our Lord's Passion. One of the saddest facts recorded in the New Testament is the hostility of organized religion to Jesus. Pharisaism, for example, the very syllables of which seem to us to imply a sneer, had as its original guiding purpose the defense of the faith against paganism and materialism, by an ardent zeal for the will of God as revealed in the Law. Yet midway in its career Pharisaism lost heart, forgot its early ideals, became reactionary, stodgy, critical of Christ, and in the end conspired with the Temple authorities to crucify the Lord of Glory. The fort had capitulated to the enemy!

"The most awful thing in the death of Jesus," Archbishop Soederblom reminds us, "is that it was brought

about by men who were following or believed themselves
to be following, good and honorable reasons for their
actions. Men of various classes, the guardians of religion
and of public morals and of the order of society itself
united to crucify Jesus. They were men like you and me."
That is why we keep Lent. That is why the Church lifts
up her voice and calls all Christians to repentance. "Turn
ye even to me with all your heart, and with fasting and
with weeping and with mourning." There is an old Passion hymn, a great favorite in Luther's day, that opens
with the question, "O thou wretched Judas, what hast
thou now done?" Fortunately the hymn is no longer sung,
for as Luther pointed out it tends to keep the Passion back
in a by-gone day as though it were none of our affair.
More to the point is the personal and deeply penitent confession of that other Passion chorale, "Who was the guilty,
who brought this upon Thee, alas *my* treason, Jesus, hath
undone Thee." He was wounded for *our* transgressions.

As we stand tonight upon the threshold of Lent our
Lord would speak to us through our text a warning against
a subtle danger that vitiates many a spiritual life. There
is a way which seemeth right unto a man, but the end
thereof is the way of death unto the spirit. In the measure
as we learn to guard against the lurking danger that besets
our religious life, we shall be set free to keep our Lent in
a positive and joyful manner.

I

Prayer, almsgiving and fasting are the three forms in which the spiritual life has chiefly manifested itself. In Jewish lore prayer was conceived of as a duty man owed God, almsgiving a duty man owed his fellow man, and fasting a duty one owed oneself. Christ Himself, need we say it, engaged in all three. Between the first act of His public ministry as He came streaming from the waters of His baptism, lifting up His heart in prayer, and the closing act of that same ministry three years later when He breathed out His young life upon a cross in an evening prayer He had been taught as a child, "Father into thy hands I commend my spirit," He had by day, and through the long watches of the night, engaged in prayer unceasing. That He also fasted is testified by the dramatic first temptation which terminated the forty days' fast in the wilderness. And His whole life was an almsgiving: He gave Himself unsparingly.

How surprising it is then, to hear Jesus, in the Sermon on the Mount, of which our text is a portion, utter such stern warnings against the dangers that attend prayer, fasting and almsgiving. Be not as the hypocrites! Do you see this man? "He's fasting," you say. You can tell it by the lorn, pinched look on his face. And if you examine more closely you may even discover the cautious use of cosmetics to emphasize the hollow eye, the hollow cheek. In passing, Jesus points out another man in the act of bestowing a coin upon a beggar. He had chosen the psychological moment to do it. People saw it and applauded. People heard about it. It was like a fanfare of trumpets at a parade. And yet a third man comes under our Lord's scrutiny. He is engaged in prayer. Like some miser gloating over his golden hoard, caressing each coin in turn, this man counts his many shining virtues, names them one by one. "God, I thank thee that I am not as the rest of men, extortioners, unjust, adulterers. . . . I fast. . . . I give tithes." What ailed these three? The Great Physician lay a diagnostic finger upon the evil in those good deeds which like a cunning thief broke through and stole their worth. The end of their religious exercises was not to glorify God and enjoy Him forever, but to glorify themselves and enjoy the applause of men as long as it would last. Their true purpose was not to advance the Kingdom but to enhance their own good names and reputations. And so, in aspiring to be religious heroes they became in reality, religious humbugs, hypocrites.

Like a volatile perfume whose sweet odor escapes when exposed to the air, leaving only the empty form that enclosed it, the spirit of religion easily evaporates leaving only the empty form, "full of sound and fury, signifying nothing." Instead of being a service unto God who is of purer eyes than to behold iniquity it then becomes a mere form, a show. Old J. S. Bach used to write over the scores of his amazing chorale preludes the words "Soli Deo

Gloria." Would that every musician who enters into the courts of the Lord could do likewise. Who is there, charged with the responsibility of leading public prayer, that must not admit at times of being more conscious of the people "out there" than of the One above. We smile wistfully over the news report of a certain prayer as being "the most eloquent prayer ever offered to a Boston audience." Indeed! The King in "Hamlet" was honest enough to admit, "My words rise up, my thoughts remain below." Would that we were equally candid with ourselves.

As a religious group the Pharisees have long since gone to their reward, but Pharisaism has not passed away, for the spirit of Pharisaism is the pride that apes humility. Someone has well said, "It is possible for the devout to be proud of his piety, for the prayerful to be proud of his supplication . . . , for the fasting to be proud of his fasts, for the donor to be proud of his gifts, for the penitent to be proud of his penitence, for the lowly to be proud of his lowliness. . . ." With one lancetlike word, Jesus probed beneath all externals and outward appearances . . . , beneath all forms and ceremonies, beneath our ostentatious goings and givings, beneath all looks and professions, beneath all self-advertising words and works. Penetrating to the very quick and marrow of our inner truer, secret selves, He said, "Blessed are the poor in spirit." "Be not as the hypocrites, of a sad countenance: for they disfigure their faces that they may appear unto men to fast."

In that candid self-revelation, his "Autobiography," Benjamin Franklin writes, "In reality, there is, perhaps no one of our natural passions so hard to subdue as pride. Disguise it, struggle with it, beat it down, stifle it, mortify it as much as one pleases, it is still alive, and will every now and then peep out and show itself. . . . Even if I should conceive that I had completely overcome it, I should probably be proud of my humility."

Is it possible, then, for a man to escape this shadow, this vain show that goes in and out with him? Can we tear off the mask of conscious or unconscious make-believe? In one of Eugene O'Neill's strange plays, each character is provided with a mask which he hastily slips over his countenance whenever another character enters the room, but as soon as he is left alone again the mask is dropped and the character becomes himself once more. Thus would the playwright remind us that since all the world's a stage and the men and women players, we are truly "in character" only when we are alone. Religion, as a famous definition has it, is what we do with our solitude. If we are never solitary we are never religious. No wonder then that Christ prescribes solitude as a curative for our ailing religious lives. When you pray, Christ says, Shut the door. Then we shall stop making words, we shall cease turning neat phrases, we shall begin conversing with God unto whom all hearts are open and from whom no secrets are hid. When you give alms, counsels Christ, do

it by stealth; don't even let your left hand know what
your right hand is about. Then we may be sure our mo-
tives are pure. When you fast, says Christ, keep it hidden
from the view of men by a bright morning face and a
head anointed as though you were off to a banquet.

> "O Thou, to Whose all-searching sight
> The darkness shineth as the light,
> Search, prove my heart; it pants for Thee;
> O burst these bonds, and set it free.
>
> "Wash out its stains, refine its dross;
> Nail my affections to the Cross;
> Hallow each thought; let all within
> Be clean as Thou, my Lord, art clean."

Emerson said, "Every man alone is sincere." Lent offers
us the opportunity to be alone with our thoughts before
the Cross. Lent calls us to survey the wondrous Cross, and
pour contempt on all our pride. Then, and there, if ever,
we will pray in the words of the Ash Wednesday collect:
"Create and make in us new and contrite hearts."

II

In the measure that Lent delivers us from preoccupa-
tion with ourselves which is the meaning of pride and the
root of sin, we are enabled to keep our Lent with profit
both to ourselves and our needy brother. For if, in utter
sincerity we do indeed turn to God with all our hearts, and
rend our hearts and not our garments, God will give us a

new spirit and new tasks and responsibilities. Instead of feeding our egos we shall find a world in need of daily bread, yea and in need of that which bread alone cannot satisfy. Instead of pleasing ourselves with high-sounding prayers we shall be bowed with the burden of all this weary unintelligible world. We shall perforce fall "with all our weight of cares upon the great world's altar stairs that slope through darkness up to God."

Our text speaks particularly of fasting. "When ye fast," says Christ. Now fasting is a custom whose observance has all but disappeared in evangelical circles, and there is sufficient evidence that even in the Roman Church it is kept with unswerving fidelity by only the minority of the faithful. Moreover we may ask with Robert Herrick

> "Is this a fast, to keep
> The larder lean?
> And clean
> From fat of veals and sheep?
>
> "Is it to quit the dish
> Of flesh, yet still
> To fill
> The platter high with fish?
>
> "Is it to fast an hour
> Or ragg'd to go,
> Or show
> A downcast look and sour?
>
> "No: 'Tis a fast to dole
> Thy sheaf of wheat,
> And meat,
> Unto the hungry soul.

"It is to fast from strife,
From old debate
And hate;
To circumcise thy life.

"To show a heart grief-rent;
To starve thy sin,
Not bin;
And that's to keep thy Lent."

"Fasting and almsgiving are linked together in the Gospel. For giving from one's surplus requires no sacrifice. True love gives not of its abundance but by depriving itself, by fasting. To consider the fasting which Christ speaks of in the Sermon on the Mount merely as religious self-discipline, as self-castigation, is utterly to misunderstand its nature and purpose. The Sermon on the Mount never halts at the individual and his righteousness; ever and everywhere it presses on from the individual to the group, from the 'I' to the 'Thou.' In Jesus' Gospel, fasting is self-discipline in the sense of willing obedience and response to the all-constraining love of Christ, in service to God and neighbor. Why did Jesus begin His ministry with a forty-day fast? That He might perform exercises of religious self-castigation? Certainly not. It was, for Him, an expression of perfect devotion to the Father's Will in His mission."

Hunger stalks the earth today as it has not done within living memory. How many millions will have starved to death before the war is over we do not know, and the mind shrinks from making the dread surmise. When once the war is over, we who have been the arsenal of death, we who have provided the torch for burning, must then supply the plow for tilling and the seed for planting, and in sober prose "to dole thy sheaf of wheat, and meat, unto the hungry soul." Shall we not, for Christ's sweet sake, perform with cheerfulness and love that which for patriotism we are now doing for purposes of death and destruction?

In the measure that we thus keep our Lent we shall find the Cross no intolerable burden, but shall discover the hidden bliss in the paradox of today's Gospel. He who fasts for Christ's sake presents no sad countenance to the world. Rather he anoints his head and washes his face for joy. And he who gives himself with his alms is not the loser, for he is laying up treasure where the corroding hand of time nor the grasping hand of thieves can ever reach. "He who will live for himself shall have small troubles but they will seem to him great. He who will live for others shall have great troubles, but they will seem to him small." And as another has testified, he who will carry the cross shall find it indeed a burden, but such a burden as wings are to a bird, or sails are to a ship.

Let me close by bringing you the story of an old farmer and his wife who lived on a little patch of ground high up on the moors of Finland. In the fall the old farmer had tilled the soil and sowed his wheat. During the winter the snow covered the tender wheat with a soft warm blanket. But when the spring came torrential rains swept away the crop, leaving very little to grow unto the harvest. To his wife's despairing cry the farmer gave answer, "God is only testing us, not forsaking." He instructed her to eke out the flour for baking bread by mixing it with an equal amount of coarse bark. He himself traded stock for seed, worked doubly hard, ploughed the fields and scattered the good seed on the ground, and prayed to God for the increase. But the next year disaster again stalked the fields. Hail cut down the standing grain. To his wife's complaining refrain the farmer replied, "The Lord is only testing us, not forsaking." Again he instructed her to mix bark with the white flour, while he redoubled his efforts in the fields and prayed to God for the harvest. And so the third year came the abundant harvest. Joyfully the farmer told his wife, "You see, God was only testing us, not forsaking." Joyfully the farmer's wife replied, "Yes, now I can throw away the old coarse flour and bake pure white bread once more!" But the old farmer shook his head, and taking his wife by the hand, said, "Good wife, only they stand the test who do not forget their needy brethren! Mix coarse bark with the fine white flour yet this year, for the frost has destroyed our neighbor's crop!" "To dole thy sheaf of wheat, and meat unto the hungry soul, to show a heart grief-rent; to starve thy sin, not bin; and that's to keep thy Lent!" Amen.

Invocavit

CHRIST OUR SINLESS SAVIOUR

FRANK H. CLUTZ

Trinity Church

GERMANTOWN, PHILADELPHIA, PENNSYLVANIA

The Proper Gospel for

INVOCAVIT

Then was Jesus led up of the spirit into the wilderness to be tempted of the devil. And when he had fasted forty days and forty nights, he was afterward an hungered. And when the tempter came to him, he said, If thou be the Son of God, command that these stones be made bread. But he answered and said, It is written, Man shall not live by bread alone, but by every word that proceedeth out of the. mouth of God. Then the devil taketh him up into the holy city, and setteth him on a pinnacle of the temple, and saith unto him, If thou be the Son of God, cast thyself down: for it is written, He shall give his angels charge concerning thee: and in their hands they shall bear thee up, lest at any time thou dash thy foot against a stone. Jesus said unto him, It is written again, Thou shalt not tempt the Lord thy God. Again, the devil taketh him up into an exceeding high mountain, and showeth him all the kingdoms of the world, and the glory of them; and saith unto him, All these things will I give thee, if thou wilt fall down and worship me. Then saith Jesus unto him, Get thee hence, Satan: for it is written, Thou shalt worship the Lord thy God, and him only shalt thou serve. Then the devil leaveth him, and, behold, angels came and ministered unto him.
—MATTHEW 4: 1-11.

CHRIST OUR SINLESS SAVIOUR

BECAUSE of Christ's victory over Satan in the wilderness temptation and in every succeeding hour of trial, He has been acclaimed sinless. To no other person has perfection ever been attributed. In all the world's history there has never been made and sustained a claim of sinlessness for any man save Jesus Christ.

The first man of the race, though created sinless, was faced with the all important choice between good and evil. He decided in favor of evil and sin. Moses, the lawgiver, was forbidden entrance into the Holy Land and died for his disobedience. Confucius, founder of one of the world's leading religions, wrote: "In letters I am perhaps equal to other men; but the character of the perfect man, carrying out in his conduct what he professes, is what I have not yet attained to." In the Koran, Mohammed is commanded to pray for his sins. There is in Buddhism no thought of claiming absolute purity for Buddha.

Jesus stands alone in this quality. He is absolutely unique here. Nothing about him impressed more deeply his early followers. John, for one, writes: "There is no unrighteousness in him." Peter calls Him "a lamb without blemish and without spot." In Hebrews, He is described as "holy, harmless, undefiled and separate from sinners." What shall we say of such claims? If they rest on truth and not on falsehood, they make Him the Sinless One.

Repeating Christ's own question to ourselves as present-day disciples, we ask "What think ye of Christ?" What are we thinking of Him these days? Is He our Sinless Saviour? To see His sinlessness rising out of and above the struggles with the evil one, is to know that He understands and sympathizes with us in our own struggles. We are given assurance when we remember this of Him, "In all points tempted like as we are, yet without sin."

There is much to be gained from an earnest meditation on Christ's temptation experience. Its reality needs to be borne in mind and the way in which His trials make Him brother to us in ours. Jesus Christ is no Saviour for us, if He knew no struggles like ours. In the wilderness, therefore, we must realize that His humanity was fully expressed, His humiliation was genuine. This battle with the devil has no significance unless it was in earnest. It was. It was a real temptation; as real as yours and mine. His own report of what occurred evidences a vivid reality.

I—*Times of Temptation*

He was tempted, "like as we are." Comparing His temptations and ours we know that this is true. We find that our greatest temptations come in time of our greatest power and strength, not in weakness and inadequacy. This is true in all life's experience. Greater ability, greater responsibility, or greater name all mean increased possibility for misuse or abuse. Larger power and influence tend always toward unfair advantage. The successful and able lawyer is presented many possible avenues for wrong action which never come to an unknown brother in the profession. It has been truly said that "Great temptations keep company with great powers" and "A typhoon is impossible in a teacup."

Witness this very thing in Jesus' experience at His baptism. He received the blessing of the Father who said, "This is my well-beloved Son" and the Holy Spirit came to Him. We read that He was almost immediately "led up of the Spirit into the wilderness to be tempted." What was the temptation that came to God's Son, so recently pronounced such by God Himself? "If thou be the Son of God—." There it is—a challenge to His very nature as revealed at the baptism. The time of trial, often, is the time of power and strength.

Another season of temptation comes when we are alone, or faced with self. There are personal life problems which bring great testings. We are prone to feel that most of men's downfalls are due to the influence and leadings of the crowds and companions. But the most deciding and deepest issues of life are determined when a man is dealing with self and the dedication of self. This very thing is what some people most fear. The way of victory is, however, in the direction of facing the battle and fighting through to the conquest of evil and the triumph of right. Jesus went alone into the wilderness and won in the contest what must be determined in his own consciousness. It was His own temptation and each of us has his own.

Do temptations come once and then forever disappear? Have we found it so, and did Jesus? There is in life no such occasional or final experience. We must remind ourselves that it is incorrect to speak of "The temptation of Jesus," as though it was all over after the victory in the wilderness. Rather do we remember that "The devil departed for a season." There were many returns, as in Peter's objection to the Master's prophecy of His death and in the Gethsemane prayer time.

Like Him, we learn that we are never through with temptations. As long as we are living and growing, we shall have them. Nor is this without purpose and benefit. In each victory won we grow stronger and more steadfast. Over some temptations we may win almost perfect and complete victory, but others will take their place. Life is a field on which the contest continues and each time the tempter is foiled the Christian grows in strength and truth.

Our temptations may, then, be to us a blessing instead of a curse. We know that when we pray, "Lead us not into temptation," we really ask our Father for strength to overcome rather than for freedom from temptation. "God, indeed tempts no one to sin; but we pray in this petition that He would so guard and preserve us, that the devil, the world, and our own flesh, may not deceive us, nor lead us into error and unbelief, despair, and other great and shameful sins; and, that, though we may be thus tempted, we may nevertheless finally prevail and gain the victory."

Temptation is not sin. If so, Jesus would have been guilty of sinning. He knew no sin, but endured many temptations; more than we shall ever know. They are natural to man on his earthly journey. Our Lord, becoming one with man in nature, knew this too. We must recognize the inevitability of temptations and their service as a discipline toward greater strength. Let us pray, not for decreasing temptations, but for increasing power to overcome the same.

II—The Way of Victory

Jesus knew the way of victory. He drew upon a source of supreme power and the devil was defeated repeatedly. That source was God, His Father, and devotion to His Will and Word.

Here in the wilderness we have a testing of the Saviour's powers, recently given Him from on high. How are they to be used? Will it be for selfish purposes and for personal glory? What happened in the wilderness determined the question in favor of complete service to God and man. He is dedicated wholly to His Father and His fellow men. In this sense of dedication there is also the consciousness of communion with God. His Father is with Him. "The groundstone of His whole self-consciousness is the undisturbed sense of communion with God."

The temptations that Jesus knew were the same in character which Satan directs at every man. They issued from the fact that He was both divine and human. In the wilderness it was our Saviour's human side that was being attacked. This was really a struggle as to which was to rule Him and His life purposes: the natural appetites and desires or the spiritual aims and devotions. How well this conflict is known to us. With Paul we confess, "For the flesh lusteth against the Spirit, and the Spirit against the flesh; and these are contrary the one to the other." This is the ageless conflict.

Satan's first attempt to overcome Jesus was well timed. After fasting forty days and forty nights—no food or drink in all that time, he offered the suggestion that God's Son, if He is really God's Son, should be justified in satisfying His hunger by making bread of stones. Men have gone to almost unbelievable extremes to gain food in dire hunger, and the Master truly hungered. But He would not distrust His Father's care. "It is written, Man shall not live by bread alone, but by every word that proceedeth out of the mouth of God." This determination to trust

Himself to the Father remained uppermost to the very end, even as He later said: "My meat is to do the will of him that sent me."

In the second temptation Jesus was taken to the pinnacle of the temple in the holy city. He was reminded that according to the scriptures God will provide protecting care for His own. The tempter misquoted when he omitted the phrase "in thy ways" which is the condition upon which the promise was to be fulfilled. The Saviour refused to distrust God and said, "Again it is written, Thou shalt not tempt the Lord thy God." The third temptation, in the order of St. Matthew's record, was a proposal that the kingdoms of the world as viewed from the high mountain would be yielded to the Saviour if He will bow down and worship Satan. Our Lord would not disobey His Father God, but with continued devotion to His will dismissed the evil suggestion with the words, "Get thee hence, Satan; for it is written, Thou shalt worship the Lord thy God, and him only shalt thou serve."

Thus it was that in the three-fold temptation, Jesus Christ proved victor over the evil one. All that the "prince of this world" had attempted in order to bring Him into sin had failed. His triumph was complete. As John wrote concerning this experience, "All that is in the world, the lust of the flesh, and the lust of the eyes, and the pride of life, is not of the Father, but of the world."

All these had been brought to bear on Christ and had been rejected.

We must remember that He suffered thus for us. Luther wrote, "The Lord, who is mighty in battle, engaged in this conflict not for His own sake but for mine, that I might receive a lesson of faith, and learn for my encouragement that the Saviour's victory is my own by faith. Be not dismayed when thou art tempted. The Holy Spirit does not permit thee to pass thy time in indolence, but suffers temptations to approach thee that the trial of thy 'faith might be found unto praise and honor and glory at the appearing of Jesus Christ,' and that God's strength may be made perfect in thy weakness. Look to Christ; 'be not afraid, only believe.' See how the serpent's head is here bruised, and learn to trust thy heavenly friend."

Our victories must come in this way. To attempt to stand alone is to fall. To rely on the Word of God and His Eternal Truth is to be assured of the Saviour's help. He understands because of His own experience. As in His case; we are assured of divine assistance. "God is faithful, who will not suffer you to be tempted above that ye are able; but will with the temptation also make a way to escape, that ye may be able to bear it."

> "O Thou, once tempted like as we,
> Thou knowest our infirmity;
> Be Thou our Helper in the strife.
> Be Thou our true, our inward Life."

III—Blessings That Follow

The concluding words of our text describe the way in which Jesus, the Sinless Christ, defeated the devil who then departed. Immediately angels came and gave Him their blessed ministrations. The struggle over and the victory won, He was to know great peace and joy. Is there anything in human emotion to compare with this? Every true follower of Christ has sometime shared these and knows the blessings of the triumph hour.

The opposite experience has many times been ours in defeat, because we have too often yielded to temptation. "He was tempted like as we are, yet without sin." Yes, we have the same temptations, but are guilty of weakness and sin. The knowledge we have gained through our failures should spur us on to closer and more constant communion with God. What sadness follows our defeat! To yield is to bring sin and woe. Misery and grief come. Life is full of shame and despair. To Christ in His sinlessness we come with a prayer for His help. "In that he has suffered, being tempted, he is able to succor them that are tempted."

Christ's victory over temptation and every evil influence assures our victory. He emerged from the wilderness full of power and courage and continued His life in sinlessness. Never could the evils of the world undo or defeat Him. Though He was at last taken captive, tried, condemned and crucified, our Sinless Saviour overcame

sin and the grave and now lives and reigns to all eternity.
With Him and His help, we too shall conquer in the strife!

"Christian, dost thou see them
On the holy ground,
How the hosts of darkness
Compass thee around?
Christian, up and smite them,
Counting gain but loss;
Smite them by the merit
Of the holy Cross.

"Christian, dost thou hear them,
How they speak thee fair:
'Always fast and vigil?
Always watch and prayer?'
Christian, answer boldly,
'While I breathe, I pray.'
Peace shall follow battle,
Night shall end in day." Amen.

Reminiscere

GREAT FAITH

RALPH C. ROBINSON
St. Paul's Church
SPRING GROVE, PENNSYLVANIA

The Proper Gospel for

REMINISCERE

Then Jesus went thence, and departed into the coasts of Tyre and Sidon. And, behold, a woman of Canaan came out of the same coasts, and cried unto him, saying, Have mercy on me, O Lord, thou son of David; my daughter is grievously vexed with a devil. But he answered her not a word. And his disciples came and besought him, saying, Send her away; for she crieth after us. But he answered and said, I am not sent but unto the lost sheep of the house of Israel. Then came she and worshipped him, saying, Lord, help me. But he answered and said, It is not meet to take the children's bread, and to cast it to dogs. And she said, Truth, Lord: yet the dogs eat of the crumbs which fall from their master's table. Then Jesus answered and said unto her, O woman, great is thy faith: be it unto thee even as thou wilt. And her daughter was made whole from that very hour.

—MATTHEW 15: 21-28.

GREAT FAITH

IN this life man and God best meet on terms of faith. In his great chapter on faith the writer of the letter to the Hebrews says, "Without faith it is impossible to please God: for he that cometh to God *must believe that he is, and that he is a rewarder of them that diligently seek him.*" The practical goal of all worship is to strengthen man's faith in God, that God may work His works in man. Here in the Gospel for today we have a striking example of what faith can mean in a person's life. In one act of worship this distressed mother overcame the inertia of her discouragement, wiped out the obstacle of racial prejudice, focused the healing power of God upon her unfortunate daughter, and forced from the lips of the Great Physician the crowning tribute, *"Great faith."*

Here we have the kind of faith that Jesus said could move mountains. Only on one other occasion is it recorded that He described anyone's faith as being great, and that was when an officer in the army of an aggressor nation came to him on behalf of his sick servant. What is this power that can command God and harness the boundless resources of Heaven?

It would seem, first of all, that great faith has something to do with man's will to believe. This woman, whatever her limitations, had the will to believe. She was confident that Jesus was able to help her. It was her faith in Jesus that put iron into her determination. She believed with the unerring instinct of her suffering soul that Jesus had the power to command health to the diseased and tortured mind of her child. Boldly, therefore, she brushed aside the social conventions that would have prevented her, a woman, from speaking to this strange Man. Bravely she faced the displeasure of His annoyed disciples who were all for sending her away. Persistently, and with the skill of the desperate, she plead her cause before the Lord of life. In utter humility, willing to be classed with the dogs, she laid siege to Divine Love. Like Jacob of old she would not give up or let go until the blessing she sought was granted. Christ saw the travail of her soul and satisfied it with the words that set her daughter free, "Be it unto thee even as thou wilt." Out of the deep insight of a great healing ministry Dr. Grenfell has written, "It is not extraordinary that we must begin with faith. No faith, no business; no faith, no fun; no faith, no victory. The will to believe is basic to all men. . . . Christ said, 'Follow me and you shall have the light of life'."

There is a suggestion here that great faith also has something to do with the will of God. "Be it unto thee *even as thou wilt.*" Do these words mean that man can command God? Jesus said, "All things, whatsoever ye shall ask in prayer, believing, ye shall receive." Here is a great mystery, a paradox of divine grace, for which nothing on earth gives an adequate explanation. But the evidences of Scripture abound to show that mere man, through faith, communicated by prayer, can bring down the resources of Heaven to serve his will. If the forces of nature, by obedience to nature's laws, can be turned to the good of man it is not unreasonable to believe that nature's God, whom Jesus has taught men to call "Our Father," can be persuaded in our favor when we have met the conditions of the supernatural. We must not think of God as an annoyed Friend who can be coaxed to change His mind even though our requests are childish and selfish. He is the heavenly Father who delights to answer the prayers of His children when they come to Him in complete faith. "He is able to do exceeding abundantly above all that we can ask or think," says St. Paul. If we don't believe *that*, we are lost. If we do believe it, we can face the loss of all things.

"O woman, great is thy faith." How this story shames us for our *little* faith! When the church historians a hundred years from now write their appraisal of this generation they must mark at least one chapter with the word, "*apostate*"—departed from the faith. The desperate plight of the world today is due primarily not to what man has done to man but what man has done to God. We have

tried to isolate Him somewhere beyond the stars as though
He were not concerned with what is going on here in the
earth. Anyhow, we didn't need Him very much. Look
how man has grown! Yes, we have deified man and hu-
manized God to the extent that many today see little difference between "the people" and God. God is the people.
The people is God. And for that we have wars and rumors
of wars.

Our faithlessness is our greatest sin against God. We
don't believe in Him as we ought. We have too many
other conflicting loyalties we are loath to sacrifice. We
display our might as a nation with great parades but the
Kingdom of God and His righteousness still remain a
second choice. We can marshall military power such as
the world has never seen but how feebly we can demonstrate the power of God. We have magnificent churches
but no magnificent obsession. The so-called return to
religion will be nothing more than shallow sentiment
until the timid, half-hearted, wishful-thinking effort of
men's souls is overcome by something of the desperation
that drove that heathen woman to the feet of Jesus. To
find ourselves at our wit's end is no tragedy if it brings us
to the feet of Jesus. As this man-made civilization crum-
bles beneath our feet God is offering to us all that we
have sought, and more, but upon His terms—the complete surrender to His will. If the pain and suffering of
these times is to be something more than a cosmic catas-

trophe then it must lead men to a new appraisal of God and His power to redeem a lost world.

Our world, like the daughter of that woman, is "grievously vexed of the devil" and in danger of destroying itself. Yet on the word of Christ Himself it is not the will of the heavenly Father that we should perish. If we will be saved it will be by a renewal of our faith in the love of God. This is the great duty this prodigal generation owes to God—to accept Him as the Lord and Father of mankind, who through Jesus Christ has offered eternal salvation to all, sealing it with the blood of the Cross. Standing amid the ruins of an old world He offers to help us build a new and better one. It's all there—the prophet's vision, the statesman's dream, the people's hope—all there for the asking. God's will is waiting on man's. How much do we desire a new and better world? How desperate is our need? How far will we go to break ourselves of those conventions and habits that would separate us from God? How much are we willing to brave the discouragement and scorn of this impatient generation? How ready are we to humble ourselves before the Son of Man and say with that desperate woman from the coasts of Tyre and Sidon, "Lord, help me"?

O why are we so slow of heart to believe Him who said, "All power is given unto me in heaven and earth"? Why are we satisfied with the crumbs of life when the spread table and the overflowing cup are within the reach of every soul? Why are we so slow to ask, to seek, to knock, when the omnipotent Father is waiting to anoint us with His "unsearchable riches"? One word can silence all doubts, dispel all fears and break the chains of our human bondage. *Believe!* Believe on the Lord Jesus Christ! Believe that He is all pardon! Believe that He is all health! Believe that He is all peace! *There is a faith that overcomes the world!*

For some of us one of the most thrilling stories St. Luke tells in his Gospel is that related in the fifth chapter. All night the disciples had toiled with their nets and had come home empty-handed. When day broke Jesus found them wearily cleaning their nets. After He had talked to them awhile He told them to get into their boat and try again. Peter, with amazement in his voice, said, "We have toiled all night and taken nothing." Then, like swelling of an incoming tide faith began to rise in the soul of this hardy fisherman. Cutting short his temptation to argue failure for such a proposal he turned to Jesus and said, "Nevertheless, at thy word we will let down the nets." You know the rest of that great story. What a day for men to remember.

Like those weary and discouraged disciples of old we are holding empty nets today. Failure is written in large letters over our age. But the cause of man is not lost. God is in the midst of His creation. The Master is still here. He walks our desolate shores and cries to all who will hear His voice, "Launch out into the deep and let down your nets." Faith, great faith, is the answer to our discouraged and troubled souls. He who will say to God, "Nevertheless, at thy word, we will let down the nets," will not return with empty hands. He who will persist, and step by step surmount—yea, *mount up,* ever higher, ever nearer, never hesitating, like the woman of this Gospel, is bound to hear and receive the Divine Answer.

Oculi

THE FINGER OF GOD

G. E. SWOYER, D.D.
First Church
MANSFIELD, OHIO

The Proper Gospel for

OCULI

*And he was casting out a devil, and it was dumb. And it
came to pass, when the devil was gone out, the dumb spake; and
the people wondered. But some of them said, He casteth out
devils through Beelzebub the chief of the devils. And others,
tempting him, sought of him a sign from heaven. But he, knowing their thoughts, said unto them, Every kingdom divided against
itself is brought to desolation; and a house divided against a
house falleth. If Satan also be divided against himself, how shall
his kingdom stand? because ye say that I cast out devils through
Beelzebub. And if I by Beelzebub cast out devils, by whom do
your sons cast them out? therefore shall they be your judges.
But if I with the finger of God cast out devils, no doubt the
kingdom of God is come upon you. When a strong man armed
keepeth his palace, his goods are in peace: but when a stronger
than he shall come upon him, and overcome him, he taketh from
him all his armour wherein he trusted, and divideth his spoils.
He that is not with me is against me: and he that gathereth not
with me scattereth. When the unclean spirit is gone out of a
man, he walketh through dry places, seeking rest; and finding
none, he saith, I will return unto my house whence I came out.
And when he cometh, he findeth it swept and garnished. Then
goeth he, and taketh to him seven other spirits more wicked
than himself; and they enter in, and dwell there: and the last
state of that man is worse than the first. And it came to pass, as
he spake these things, a certain woman of the company lifted up
her voice, and said unto him, Blessed is the womb that bare thee,
and the paps which thou hast sucked. But he said, Yea rather,
blessed are they that hear the word of God, and keep it.*

—LUKE 11: 14-28.

THE FINGER OF GOD

IT is impossible to account for Jesus Christ unless He is accepted as divine. Try to explain the blessed Lord on any other basis and He becomes an anvil on which countless contentious and nationalistic and atheistic hammers have been and will be smashed to smithereens. No one can lightly cast aside the adorable, miracle-working, crucified Son of God.

A group of narrow-minded and outlook-blinded ecclesiastical persons found this out one day. As St. Mark tells us they had come from the great city of Jerusalem and were perhaps intoxicated by their self-importance. They were to account for Jesus and stop His marvelous progress, but the "fly in the ointment" was that they had to face facts, and facts are stubborn things to fight down. For here a miracle had been performed. No amount of legerdemain or subtle deception could reason that fact away. Some person, man or woman, and we will call that one a man to save words, had been possessed by a devil and Jesus had cast it out. The man had been cured and stood before them healed in body and mind and now this poor, formerly dumb man was telling the crowd of the glory of God. The people believed, too, for here was factual evidence. All that the scribes and Pharisees, trekking to the scene from Jerusalem, had to account for and to do so was like accounting for one times one equals one. You cannot reason away the multiplication table. Yet these haughty, angered scribes and pharisees must somehow account for the Christ or "lose face" or prestige before all those folks.

There you see the setting for real drama. Here was a man healed and the Christ who had done the healing. The multitude of people was so won by the miracle-working Lord, the scribes and Pharisees from the great city would find it hard to convince them that Christ was an imposter. Yet on one side did stand the haughty villains of the drama, whose intense purpose was to thwart the Christ. The whole scene was full of dramatic intensity as we can see when we study:

> *The Accusation Against the Christ;*
> *The Answer of Christ;*
> *The Implications of That Answer.*

I—The Accusation Against the Christ

The scribes and Pharisees who came to undermine the holy Christ were very clever. They doubtless had been sent there by the "higher-ups" in Jerusalem and were well prepared. Evil is usually keen and knows what the scores

are. That is up to a certain point evil is brilliant, but
beyond that wrong generally fails and every murderer
leaves a clue. These religious leaders were brilliant
enough not to deny the cure of this poor dumb man possessed with a dumb devil. They, therefore, were wiser than
some of our so-called intelligentsia of today who try to
reduce all cases of demon possession to a mental condition.
This whole scene points to the fact that an actual evil
power had overcome this unfortunate person. His devil
possession was as real as flesh and blood and was more
than a mere hallucination or a neurotic on a spree. The
scribes and Pharisees saw that the man was actually healed
—cured—yet their minds were not brilliant enough to see
that Jesus had enfolded the poor fellow in His great arms
of love and had driven the devil away. In their stupidity
they tried to explain the mystery away by saying, "He
casteth out devils through Beelzebub, the chief of devils."

In that answer there was strength and there was weakness. They, by their answer, made a most favorable ad-
mission that Jesus had actually conquered that demon in
the man. The weakness was in attributing the power of
Christ to Beelzebub, the prince of devils, or the god of the
bumble-bee or of the fly. By thus speaking disrespectfully
of the miracle—a natural bit of human camouflage which
we use to knock down the success of others—they thought
to discredit Jesus with the crowd about Him. Those
ignoramuses, who thought themselves bright, must have

bristled in self-importance as they spoke, and surely they must have felt that for once they had put this Galilean agitator in His place.

That accusation presented a real problem to our Lord. Was some Portia needed to defeat those Shylocks demanding their pound of Jesus' flesh? What should Jesus do— fall down in terror and retreat like a whipped cur, whining before the lash? Tell me, where do so many people get the idea that Christianity is a matter of folded hands and pious looks? Jesus was not like that. Jesus met problems when truth was at issue, although He seldom defended Himself, as Gethsemane testifies. Brother, sister, father, mother, harassed soul, what would you do in an hour when truth is at stake? Jesus at least soon "took up arms against a sea of troubles," and we, too, should be able to give a reason for the faith that is in us. Perhaps our lukewarmness in defense is that we do not realize the terrific soul-crushing problems before us and are not sold enough on God. Jesus, who came from the Throne of Love, soon answered those critics in such a way at which future ages have marveled at His answers. When the great Abraham Lincoln needed an argument against slavery he turned to Christ's answer of "a house divided against a house." Jesus' reply was so marvelous, G. Campbell Morgan wrote of it—"No man can improve on any answer Jesus gave as to the philosophy revealed, the method adopted, or the purpose gained." No wonder the officers who were once sent to arrest the miracle-working Master came back empty handed and minds dizzy and explained away their failure with those amazing words, "Never man spake like this man."

II—*The Answer of Christ*

That Jesus was wonderful in His reply to His foes, we realize as we see His mind outthink and outguess those able men. One marvels at His ability! After all, is there anything in life more amazing than the mind of man? Behold its clever working and stand in awe before the dynamic power of a great brain as a parliamentarian marshals his laws of a procedure; or a mighty orator bewitches his audience; or a consecrated pastor hurls souls before God's Judgment Throne; or a lawyer captivates a jury! It is the mind which makes a soul great and what is above the neck is ever the most important part of a man. When you see a group of doctors hold an autopsy on the human body, you more admire the brains which make the pathological study than the gray convolutions exposed to view. And never did the human mind move more like a well-oiled, co-ordinated machine than did the mind of Jesus when He answered His foes.

a—The Folly of the Argument of the Scribes and the Pharisees

As soon as they tried to explain away the miracle of Jesus, they laid themselves wide open for a terrible beating. The Bible tells us "a word fitly spoken is like apples of gold in pictures of silver." Speech is silver, but silence is golden. Once you speak or write, it is hard to retract. *Appear in print and you may hang crepe on your name or rise to immortality.* An old adage tells us, to eat grapefruit you should keep your eyes shut and your mouth open, but to succeed in life reverse the process. It was the poet, Will Carlton, who once wrote something like this—

> "Boys flying kites,
> Haul in their white wing birds,
> But you can't do that,
> When you are flying words.
> Words unexpressed
> May sometimes fall down dead,
> But God Himself can't kill them,
> When they're said."

Nor could the Pharisees retract when once they had blurted forth their absurd explanation of Jesus' miracle that He had by the power of the devil performed His wonders. Their pretentious holiness was to be shot full of holes by the blessed Christ.

Read Jesus' answer in Moffatt's clear translation of verses seventeen and eighteen: "Any realm divided against itself comes to ruin, house after house falls down; if Satan is indeed divided against himself, how can his realm stand?" There you have it. If Jesus' power was from Satan, why should He fight Himself? It would be like an army destroying its own defenses, food, and ammunition.

Even Satan was not so dumb as that. The devil does not destroy his own children. Jesus appealed that they should either say He was corrupt and His works corrupt or He was good and His works worthy ones. As Jesus reasoned away, those religious leaders had no reply.

Jesus by His response taught Christians they, too, can answer their cynical foes; for God Himself is constantly answering His enemies. On the very spot where the clever agnostic, Robert Ingersol, wrote his famous lecture, *The Mistakes of Moses,* Dr. Truett, of Dallas, Texas, tells us there is now a church of God ever preaching the saving Gospel. What an answer to the man who taught that in a few years there would not be a Bible or a Christian left! In a thousand ways, yes a billion of them, history shows on its recorded pages that there is a God and that constantly He thunders forth His answers to His critics and as time marches on ever demonstrates there is a God. Jesus soon shut the blatant mouths of those critics. Some-one said that there are certain fountain pens which run more freely just before they run out of ink. The scribes and Pharisees had run out of ink after they had run out their words and they had no "comeback" to the paralyzing blows of our God.

b—Jesus Shows the Inconsistency of Their Criticism

Jesus had yet more to say to shatter the cocksure complacency of those religious devils. He further argued that if the casting out of demons was such a reprehensible act, then that put His accusers in a ridiculous dilemma. Jesus said, verse nineteen, "And if I by Beelzebub cast out devils, by whom do your sons cast them out? therefore shall they be your judges." Ah, there he had them! Various ones in that day claimed to be exorcists and were applauded for their victories over evil spirits. When, therefore, Jesus was attacked for His success, those inconsistent deluders thrust at all who claimed to have power over demons, even their own sons or pupils. Jesus, thus by a few well-uttered words, pierced the covered sores of their hypocrisy and let the odorous refuse flow forth to view.

c—Jesus' "Finger-of-God" Explanation

After Jesus had showed the absurdity of their interpretation of His miracle and had with devastating effect smashed their statements, He next gave the explanation of His power. "Since I do not cast out devils by Beelzebub, I must cast them out by the *Finger of God*. That means, therefore, that the Kingdom of God is upon you."

By the "Finger of God," Jesus meant the spirit and the power of God. All the precious influence of God as revealed in the past, His holy part in history, His working out the salvation for the human race, His choice of Israel as the select people, the sending of the Messiah to earth, all of these were by the power of God. Now that "The Finger of God" was evidenced among them, why did they not see and hear and know and follow that power? The very miracle He had just performed was not by the power of Beelzebub but by the holy power of God. There it was, *The Finger of God* pointing at God's holy Kingdom, but they could not see it. It was, therefore, too bad for them.

What a potent argument it was! There was no way to upset His conclusions, for like a two-edged sword our Lord laid open the falsity of their attacks. Those ecclesiastical critics could only escape in confusion. They could not and neither can anyone long deny the presence and power of *The Finger of God* in life. His arguments are unfailing and His proof unanswerable. "The whole creation thunders the Ten Commandments." Each star and each proton are immersed in a moral solution. God's answers are eternally old and His proofs more ancient than the rocks. God's answers reach from Creation through Eden to Calvary and then on to the Judgment Day. Therefore, read His answers in the sky and on the sea and on the lake and in the sunsets, and follow God. Otherwise, one may look as passion- and hate-drunk as did those self-intoxicated scribes and Pharisees who were reeling down the streets of the Kingdom of God and were unable to know where they were or to realize they were passing up the Son of God, their Messiah forever.

III—*The Implications of That Answer*

Study that theme of Jesus and follow it to the utmost ramifications. The Finger of God! The Spirit of the Almighty! The Power of the Eternal! There lies the strength of the life of our Lord. He who was God had power from God. One key may unlock a box where there are many keys to unlock all other treasure chests. Know the Finger of God and you can solve all the problems of deviled humanity. Surely Christ's Word shows us that

a—Evil Is Strong and the Beleaguered Human Soul and Society, too, Are Lost Without the Help of God!

Jesus pictures that with words which sear into the human brain. A strong man owns a castle but let a stronger one come and the first man loses his castle and his possessions are scattered. We dare not let the castle of the soul be empty either, for not only does nature abhor a vacuum but so does God. Let an empty space come into the soul, even by casting out evil ideas and if you do not fill that soul with God's own constructive content, a devil seeking a habitation may move in. Not only does Satan move in, but he brings along his relatives until seven other devils more evil than the leader take over the soul.

It is all a graphic picture of the soul of a man and assures him the way to peace is not in self but in God. To trust in self-righteousness for salvation, or in baskets of food given to the poor, or "I'm as good as any Christian, so why go to church?" argument, is to open the way for any number of devils to enter a life. There are not enough eyes in all the potatoes ever given to the poor to enable their giver to see even the entrance door to the Kingdom of God. When the Peace of God comes to the human heart through a Saviour dying on the Cross for sins' forgiveness, then is the heart full of God and all the devils in the world cannot enter that soul.

Dr. Link in his book, *The Return to Religion,* for that very reason urges all to find a place in God's holy Church. He contends that all our scientific and mechanical advances have made mankind no happier. In fact, his book informs us that "the net annual increase in mental patients in hospitals in the United States has risen to four and one-half percent and the rate is still rising." Dr. Link makes the appeal—"Religion . . . is not the refuge of the weak but the weapon of the strong. I see religion as an aggressive mode of life, by which the individual becomes the master of his environment, not its complacent victim."

Society also needs that same Presence of God to save its very soul. Today and most every day the devil and all his seven assistants have taken possession of the soul of the world. We see it when we face the problem and tragedy of war. War's source is diabolical, not divine.

We do not desire to be misunderstood here. We believe that right must be upheld and nations must be defended. For a pastor to lock his church doors to protect the church, or a layman his house to protect his family and property and yet refuse to defend in time of need a government which has protected him is about the height of inconsistency.

Having said the above so as not to be misunderstood, we now say that wars among nations should end forever-more. Jesus' picture of a strong man armed and a stronger winning out is one of war. On that basis nations have always fought and died. Isn't it time that the Finger of God method be used? The only way out of all these periodic, crazy war sprees is in the spiritual. Unless we turn to God's ways of peace, the devil of war will sooner or later come into national hearts and at once arrive the other seven devils—suspicion, chicanery, "chips on the shoulders" and then the Four Horsemen of the Apocalypse demonstrate their riding ability. The only way to peace is for nations to follow the Finger of God method and through the spiritual forces completely cast out all the war demons.

b—The Evidence of the Might of the Finger of God

When we look at the positive side of the Finger of God, we have the answer to all the needs of man. The ages somehow are on the side of truth. From the dark shadows of life we can ever—if we are in tune—hear the assuring whispers of God. Jesus not only cast a dumb devil out back there nineteen hundred years ago, but all these centuries dumb things are being cast out by the Spirit of the Almighty.

Does not society improve in many ways? When were there so many voices against hate as today? When have we more seen the futility of force to fashion hopeful futures? When has there been more of a realization that as one nation falls or succeeds all nations are affected? Who has ever seen the time when there was more emphasis on the fact that the spiritual is the way to success and happiness for mankind? Left to drift alone there do come the eight devils, but if we trust in God the dumb devils go and into hearts can come the glorious blessings of forgiveness and peace and among nations the federation of love.

There lies the real burden of the Church of God—*to fill souls with the Power of God.* But that is a world-wide burden, for all nations are now back door neighbors. There is no such thing as one to claim he is a true Christian and yet refuse to see universally. The churches around the world must hammer home the great truth of Jesus that the only way to national and personal happiness is through the power of the Finger of God.

Surely one need not go very far into Christ's words to see that while society may be topsy-turvy, each heart can have peace from besetting sin. Back of all unrest and back of all upset lives and back of all sorrow is the fact of heinous sin in the world. But God conquered sin. By the Finger of God, God won and on a Cross. Never is the power of God seen better than when a soul sinks to the knees in sorrow and repentance and rises with a strange peace living in the heart. No gold can do that! No diamonds can do that! No "work-righteousness" can do that! Nothing man can do can do that! But when a tear-stained face turns to the Cross and the Atoning Blood of a dying Saviour, the miracle of forgiveness comes and a heart in good cheer can carry on and face life in its stark reality. There, most of all, is seen the power of the Finger of God.

Dr. Bauslin, sainted leader of Hamma Divinity School at Wittenberg College, once used an illustration which enables us to see the triumphant power of the Finger of God as revealed through a Cross. A terrible sinner confessed to a priest a long series of fierce sins. The priest was shocked out of the usual complacency of priests and he would pronounce no solemn tones of forgiveness. "God's spirit will not always strive with man," said the priest. The disconsolate man left in sorrow. The priest fell into a troubled dream and there he stood at the Judgment Bar of God. A man was being tried for his sins. On one side his errors were piled and the scales went down in the balance. All seemed lost but at that moment the rustle of an angel's wings was heard. In flew an angel, having in its hands a handkerchief wet with the tears of repentance. The sins were outweighed and the man was forgiven. Then the angel said—"The sacrifices of God are a broken spirit. A broken and a contrite heart, O God, thou wilt not despise." The priest awakened and in utter horror over his harshness he went out to find the man. Finally he did find him—dead beneath a tree—but under his head was a handkerchief wet with tears.

Only a legend to be sure and yet how true! The same Jesus who drove out the demon made the blessed Sacrifice that the Finger of God might bring all of us sinners penitence, forgiveness and peace. But it cost God, the Father, until there were lines in His face. That exhibition of the Power of God on the Cross cost Jesus until He thought God had forsaken Him. But, oh, it was wonderful! Our sins are forgiven by the Sacrifice of God! By the Finger of God are we redeemed! The Finger of God and the Cross merge into one and become the strange figure of a naked man silhouetted between heaven and earth on a Cross, who is the hope of improvement for a weary world and of salvation for every soul beneath the sun.

Conclusion

The miracle was past, the critics were answered and all seemed over when a woman near by lifted up her voice and said unto Him, "Blessed is the womb that bare thee, and the paps which thou hast sucked."

But He said unto her, "Yea, rather blessed, are they that hear the word of God and keep it."

Her spirit was beautiful and her words a compliment, but religion is more than that, so Jesus said. Let all not only admire the Christ as did this woman and realize His human birth, but more let "the Finger of God" point us to the Cross and give us strength not only to hear the Word of God. *but to keep it.*

Laetare

CHRIST, THE BREAD OF LIFE

RICHARD W. ROTH
Church of the Good Shepherd
CHICAGO, ILLINOIS

The Proper Gospel for

LAETARE

After these things Jesus went over the sea of Galilee, which is the sea of Tiberias. And a great multitude followed him, because they saw his miracles which he did on them that were diseased. And Jesus went up into a mountain, and there he sat with his disciples. And the passover, a feast of the Jews, was nigh. When Jesus then lifted up his eyes, and saw a great company come unto him, he saith unto Philip, Whence shall we buy bread, that these may eat? And this he said to prove him: for he himself knew what he would do. Philip answered him, Two hundred pennyworth of bread is not sufficient for them, that every one of them may take a little. One of his disciples, Andrew, Simon Peter's brother, saith unto him, There is a lad here, which hath five barley loaves, and two small fishes: but what are they among so many? And Jesus said, Make the men sit down. Now there was much grass in the place. So the men sat down, in number about five thousand. And Jesus took the loaves; and when he had given thanks, he distributed to the disciples, and the disciples to them that were set down; and likewise of the fishes as much as they would. When they were filled, he said unto his disciples, Gather up the fragments that remain, that nothing be lost. Therefore they gathered them together, and filled twelve baskets with the fragments of the five barley loaves, which remained over and above unto them that had eaten. Then those men, when they had seen the miracle that Jesus did, said, This is of a truth that prophet that should come into the world. When Jesus therefore perceived that they would come and take him by force, to make him a king, he departed again into a mountain himself alone.

—JOHN 6: 1-15.

CHRIST, THE BREAD
OF LIFE

THE world is war conscious. Because of the terrible war that is raging, people in all walks of life are thinking, talking, and acting in terms of war; advertisers are using war mottoes for their ads; radio programs are war minded in their music, dramas and talks. Everything seems to be connected with war and its terminology.

Among the many war phrases we hear, is the "necessity of supplies." Proper and sufficient supplies are necessary to win any battle. In the courts, supplies of information, testimony, facts are needed to prove a case.

In business, supplies of merchandise and sales ability are needed to be successful.

In war, supplies of ammunition, men, food, maps, tanks, planes, ships, guns and knowledge are needed for a conquering nation.

In the battle of life, supplies are needed. There must be food, clothing, shelter. And more important there must be an ever-flowing supply of spiritual things such as inspiration, courage, balance, vitality, faith, love, hope, religion. Without such supplies the human being would starve and soon die.

In all life a constant flow of fresh and new supplies is necessary. A reservoir that is not fed with water will go dry, and as a result those who depend upon it to furnish them with water will dry up and die. Any life that is not fed with supplies of food will die. Nothing can exist without the proper life-giving supplies. A soul that is not fed with the Word of God will die. For, after all, the Word of God is the life-giving source of our strength, courage, hope and forgiveness, redemption and salvation.

Our souls must be fed constantly with the Bread of Life just as our bodies must be fed constantly to keep them alive. The Bread of Life that nourishes our souls is the Word of God. If we fail to hear it; if we neglect the Sacraments, our souls will become undernourished and will soon die.

Today there is much death and destruction. Not only are men, women, and children being killed by the thousands, but there are thousands more who are discouraged, fearful, defeated.

The world is crying for a solution to all this "Hell on earth." It is crying for deliverance from its rule of pagan leaders.

But we must not forget that the world has been given the opportunity to feed on the "Bread of Life" and has refused it. Is there any wonder that innocent men, women, and children are being tortured and killed? Is there any wonder that people have become discouraged, fearful, defeated? When man refuses to hear or follow God's Word, he must expect to suffer. And that is just what has happened. Things were going along too smoothly, people thought they didn't need God's help, and guidance. They forsook Him and His Word. The results are now felt.

But it is not too late. The Word of God says, "Turn ye from your evil ways and repent and I will heal your sick land."

Let us, let all people turn from their selfish, evil, pagan, hateful, distrustful ways and turn to God and His ways of life and then we can hope for a world of peace.

Christ realized the necessity of supplying His followers with material and spiritual food. He didn't allow the faithful ones to go hungry. He provided them with food for their bodies and souls.

In the Gospel Lesson appointed for this Fourth Sunday in Lent, we have an example of Jesus' care for those who hear His Word, those who trust in Him. A multitude of about five thousand people had been listening to Jesus' words of comfort, hope, strength and way of life for three days. For many, a long journey would have been necessary to reach their homes. They were hungry and tired. Jesus knew they needed food to sustain them. He said to Philip, "Whence shall we buy bread that these may eat?" and Philip answered, "Two hundred pennyworth of bread is not sufficient for them." Of course two hundred penny-worth, about $35.00, would not have been enough to buy food for five thousand people.

Then Andrew said, "There is a lad here who has five barley loaves and two small fishes, but what are they among so many?"

Jesus said, "Make the men sit down." And Jesus took the loaves, and when He had given thanks, He distributed to the disciples, and the disciples to them that were set down, and likewise of the fishes as much as they would. When they were filled He said unto the disciples, "Gather up the fragments that remain, that nothing be lost." Therefore they gathered them together, and filled twelve baskets with the fragments of the five barley loaves which remained over and above unto them which had eaten.

There are many lessons to learn from this great miracle. But if we learn nothing else from this story, let us learn that Jesus, out of His love for humanity, cares for all followers. He provides His followers with food to nourish their bodies and souls.

But we must be near Him; we must be in His Presence if we would receive His loving care and sustenance. Let us remember that the five thousand people he fed had been with Him for some time hearing His words of peace and love. They received His spiritual food and material food because they were in His Presence. We can't expect

God's blessings to come to us, if we do not know Him, hear Him, or come unto Him.

Jesus is our Bread of Life. Through Him all life is made possible, both present and future. It is Christ who sustains all life. "I am the way, the truth, and the life: no man cometh unto the Father but by me."

Without Christ, see what comes to the world! Satan takes over. The minds and hearts of people are filled with distrust, fear, envy, jealousy, hate, sin. The result is war and destruction. And to bring it closer to home, we find that the home which refuses the "Bread of Life"—the home that refuses to hear God's Word and live by it is broken with trouble, sadness, and shame.

It is a peculiar thing that people refuse the teachings of Christ when the world is demonstrating so well the results of following Satan. This demonstration is horrible, destructive, murderous. How long will it be until people wake up and follow Christ, the Prince of Peace? How long will it be until people forsake other gods, other powers, self, and follow the teachings of Christ which alone can solve our problems of the world? Instead of self-righteousness, greed, hate, envy, jealousy, might and power, brutality, slavery, Christ teaches love, equality, liberty, peace. How much better His teachings are. Yet, too many will not permit themselves to follow His way.

Christ is the Bread of Life. All other bread is far from life-giving. Rather it is life-taking. Satan's bread may taste good for the moment, but it brings about death, not life.

We who believe in Christ and follow His doctrines have an obligation to society—to the world. Jesus expects us to help Him distribute this "Bread of Life." He asked the disciples to give the bread and the fish to the multitude. He said, "Give them to eat." But the disciples felt they hadn't enough food to feed the great crowd of people. They felt there wasn't enough to go around. And they wanted to send the people away—hungry.

Let us remember friends, we do not solve a difficulty by ignoring it. Let us also be reminded, that Christ is able to perform miracles that are beyond our comprehension.

Too often we see a job ahead of us that should be done, but ignore it or haven't faith enough to tackle it. We cry, "Send them away." We look out on the vast field of un-churched people in America and foreign countries. We feel that we haven't enough "food," money enough, pastors enough, etc., to care for these people and so we give up in despair.

Andrew asked, "What are these among so many?" He couldn't understand how five loaves and two fishes could possibly feed five thousand people. This was a natural question. In man's way of thinking such a thing is impossible, but we forget that with God, nothing is impossible. If we would but place our impossible tasks in the hands of God and in faith do our utmost, great things would be accomplished for the Kingdom of God.

But too many of us would rather give up in defeat over the greatness of our work.

The twelve disciples, merely twelve men, set out against a whole world of pagans and accomplished their purpose with the help of God. Luther stood alone at the Diet of Worms and with the help of God accomplished His purpose.

Today, the minority of Christians are challenged by the majority of pagan unbelievers. Will we give up saying, "What are these among so many?" Certainly not, if we truly trust in God and we ourselves feed on the "Bread of Life." But let us not forget it is not enough to enjoy the food of God only for ourselves, but we must distribute this food to all people in every land.

If we would but place the small things, the minority of Christians, in the hands of God and trust in Him to develop them, we would accomplish wonders in the speeding of the word of peace to the world.

But too many of us lack that faith in Christ and His ability to do great things with small things. We too often waste the fragments that are left over. We waste our opportunities to preach the Gospel to all people. We are too content to enjoy the richness of God's Grace by ourselves. As a result we must live in a world that is torn with war, and all sorts of sadness and trouble.

And so in conclusion, let us not only feast on the "Bread of Life," furnished by Christ for those who believe in Him; but let us feed the food to all people everywhere. He alone can and does supply the world with all that is good, honorable, happy, peaceful, and hopeful. Cling to Him as your source of Life, now and forever more.

Judica

MEASURING JESUS

Walter Krumwiede, S.T.D.
Grace Church
Rochester, New York

The Proper Gospel for

JUDICA

*Which of you convinceth me of sin? And if I say the truth, why do ye not believe me? He that is of God heareth God's words: ye therefore hear them not, because ye are not of God. Then answered the Jews, and said unto him, Say we not well that thou art a Samaritan, and hast a devil? Jesus answered, I have not a devil; but I honour my Father, and ye do dishonour me. And I seek not mine own glory: there is one that seeketh and judgeth. Verily, verily, I say unto you, If a man keep my saying, he shall never see death. Then said the Jews unto him, Now we know that thou hast a devil. Abraham is dead, and the prophets; and thou sayest, If a man keep my saying, he shall never taste of death. Art thou greater than our father Abraham, which is dead? and the prophets are dead: whom makest thou thyself? Jesus answered, If I honour myself, my honour is nothing: it is my Father that honoureth me; of whom ye say, that he is your God: yet ye have not known him; but I know him: and if I should say, I know him not, I shall be a liar like unto you: but I know him, and keep his saying. Your father Abraham rejoiced to see my day: and he saw it, and was glad. Then said the Jews unto him, Thou art not yet fifty years old, and hast thou seen Abraham? Jesus said unto them, Verily, verily, I say unto you, Before Abraham was, I am. Then took they up stones to cast at him: but Jesus hid himself, and went out of the temple, going through the midst of them, and so passed by.—*JOHN 8: 46-59.

MEASURING JESUS

IF there is one obligation Jesus insists each one of us must meet, it is this—that we deliberately and carefully take His measure.

The reason for this is very plain. We cannot really come to know Him, have full faith in Him, follow Him unhesitatingly, and serve Him loyally unless we learn who and what He is, is for us, personally, and through us, for the whole world. One single fault in our estimate of Him throws out of focus, and therefore distorts our whole relationship to Him and our entire living for Him.

It is not essential that our measuring of Jesus be complete. Indeed, not all of eternity will be sufficient for us ever to come to know Him completely; but this one thing is essential that we do measure Him, and measure Him correctly. That is why Jesus, Himself, was constantly, by word and deed, asking those about Him to judge Him. He challenged judgment, not for the sake of argumentation, but to give rise to an acceptance of Himself and His claims and teachings.

It is not strange, therefore, that we find Him, as in today's Gospel Lesson, throwing down before His hearers, like a gauntlet, the challenge of His words,—"Which of you convinceth ('convicteth') me of sin?"

Here is, truly, an arresting challenge, one which calls for the fullest measuring of the One, who makes it. Its implications are so far reaching it simply cannot be avoided. It must be met. And it can be met only in one of two ways,—by the complete acceptance or the utter rejection of Jesus. This same dilemma He lays before us this morning. Answer it we must, answer it either by a confession—"Lord, I believe, help thou my unbelief"—or by a rejection—"Away with him; crucify him." Which is it to be?

Let us see how Jesus gave to His hearers that day, not only a challenge, but also the material from which to construct the answer His love for them yearned to have them give Him.

He asked them first of all to find in Him one stain of sin. "Which of you convinceth me of sin?" The prophets had told Israel to look for this sign of sinlessness in the One God would send to act as their Messiah and Mediator. This One was to be the lamb, without spot and without blemish. He might of free choice, and to save sinners, make His bed with sinners and find His grave with the wicked; but He must be in His life and living among God's people, the One altogether lovely, the One in whom no fault could be found.

This challenge Jesus threw out to those about Him.

He asked them to judge Him, to measure Him according to the standard of sinlessness God had set for Him. This same challenge Jesus throws before us today. He asks a like measuring according to God's standard of righteousness. We are to try to find in Him the stain of sin. We must look for faults in His character, in His life, in His service for God, in His contacts with us. If we can find such stain of sin, we have no alternative—He says we must refuse Him first place in our hearts and souls. If we cannot find such stain of sin in Him, again there is no alternative, we must accept Him, kneel before Him in worship, live with Him in the fellowship of faith, and serve Him daily.

Having asked His hearers to measure Him, Jesus tells them how to measure Him. It is one thing to throw down the gauntlet. It is quite another thing to show the foe how he can pick up that gauntlet with a rather certain hope of putting the challenger to utter defeat.

Jesus often did just this. He would create a dilemma, and then offer the solution, offer it in such a way that the very offer might become a reason for allegiance to Him because it bore within itself the very germs of Jesus' possible defeat.

To those about Him Jesus now says, "I have asked you to try to find some taint of sin in me. The best way for you to do this is to measure me by the truth, the truth of what I say, the truth of what I do. Do I speak the truth?

Do I bring to you exactly that which I have seen with my Father? Is my record true? If so, why do ye not believe me?"

Jesus' own estimate of a liar, whether a liar in word or in deed, was this,—that one's father could not be God; he must be the devil. Such an one was not only sinful, he was essentially devilish. Here is the measure He gives them to measure Him by.

Could Jesus really ask His hearers to make this truth test of Him? They tacitly admitted He could by the manner with which they rejected Him. The bitterness, the malice, the utter disregard of the truth by which they brought about His crucifixion is the best acknowledgment they could have made of His sinlessness and that, because He was sinless, He could say, "My record is true."

And what a record of God that was which Jesus gave to those of His day. Without diminishing God's might, beclouding His righteousness, or belittling His justice, Jesus unveiled to them God the Father, loving, merciful, gracious, yearning for and working for the sinner's return home. His record was true because it brought God down to this world without dethroning Him; true, because it showed God, merciful and gracious, without destroying His righteousness and justice; true, because it transformed the power of God into the mercy of love, so that the sinner could say, "God so loved the world, that he gave his only begotten Son, that whosoever believeth in him should not perish, but have everlasting life."

The record of Jesus' words was not only for His day: it is for our day, too: for every day in every man's life. It is being spoken by Jesus this morning just as clearly as He uttered it then to those who heard Him. Since His record of the things of God is now being spoken, it is being offered to us now. What are we going to do with this record? What is our reply to be to His words, "If I say the truth, why do ye not believe me?" We recognize darkness by the absence of light. We recognize falsehood by the absence of the truth. Light has no fellowship with darkness, nor truth with falsehood. Jesus asks us now, "Have I spoken the truth?" Our answer is what? "Yes"? —then, let us say with Thomas, "My Lord and my God."

Now it is quite possible for one to tell what is true, and yet, not be of the truth oneself. Jesus recognized this, and so He was constrained to offer not only the record of His Word, but also the record of His works. He offered to those about Him the record of His life. "I seek not mine own glory. I keep his sayings." With these words He laid before them His whole life as a ladder to climb to God.

His was not a life lived in the solitude of a hermit's cell. He lived daily and openly with and before His fellow men. In their homes and in the market places; in some small village and in Jerusalem; along the highways and on the mountain side; in synagogue and in the Temple —He was ever with them and constantly before them. And as His enemies hung on every word He uttered, seeking to trap Him through His words, so they eagerly sought Him out to watch what He did that through His deeds they might bring about His destruction.

But their eager watchfulness bore no legitimate fruit. His life was as true to truth as His record. That is why, when they brought Him to trial, only false evidence could be brought; that is why, in almost scornful contempt, His reply to them was, "I spake openly to the world; I ever taught in the synagogue, and in the temple, whither the Jews always resort; and in secret have I said nothing."

This careful and minute searching of Jesus' life did not end with the close of His earthly ministry. It is still going on. With just as much eager malice and hatred, men are trying to find in His life some taint, some weakness, for Jesus ever offers His life to mankind, offers His life as the record of truth. And He is saying just as clearly as He said then, "For what evil deed are you accusing me? Have I ever sought my own glory? Have I not always done everything good? Have I not kept His sayings?" To this record of His life an answer must be given. The question is, Will our answer be that of a believing heart and a consecrated life, or, will we, too, take up stones to cast at Him?

Someone may say, "What difference does it make

what answer I give to Jesus' challenge? I can't see that my measuring of Him can have any effect on my character and life." Ah, but it does. Read, carefully, what Jesus said to His hearers. Consider carefully what they tried to do to Him. The real menace to them lay not in their refusal of Him, or even in their attempt to stone Him. The real menace to them lay in their hearts, for what they were in their hearts, made them act toward Him as they did.

Recall Jesus' words to them—"Now ye seek to kill me, a man that hath told you the truth. Ye do the deeds of your father. If God were your Father, ye would love me? Ye are of your father the devil, and the lusts of your father ye will do: he was a murderer from the beginning, and abode not in the truth, because there is no truth in him."

A scathing denunciation? Yes. But more than this, a passionate plea to them to measure Him in such a way that they would not become guilty of the very sin toward which He so clearly saw they were inevitably heading, the sin of rejection. There is where the danger lies to those who say, "It makes little difference whether or not we measure Jesus. Our life will go on just the same." No, it will not; it cannot. Jesus, the truth, tells us so.

Jesus wants us to measure Him, that through such measuring we may be free from the sin of rejection. Every one of us will some day have to face Jesus, face Him not as we can now as the One who pleads with us; but face Him as the One who sits on the great white throne to judge. Today it is yet possible for us to measure Him so as to receive from Him only that which is good. Before the throne no such possibility will exist. Then it is no offer of grace; only a certain and fearful judgment and the passing of an irrevocable sentence.

One of the names given to this Sunday is "Judgment Sunday"—the day on which we judge ourselves as we judge Jesus. The sentence we pass on Him today is the sentence we pass upon ourselves when we come before the throne to give an account of our stewardship. The measure with which we measure Jesus, is the very measure with which we ourselves will be measured. Where are we putting ourselves now—are we acknowledging the devil as our father through our rejection of Jesus, or are we confessing God as our Father as we accept the record of Jesus' words and works and proclaim Him "Lord of our life, and God of our salvation"?

"Which of you convinceth me of sin? And if I speak and live the truth, why do ye not believe me?"

Palmarum

THE HEART'S KING

O. GARFIELD BECKSTRAND, D.D.
Trinity Church
ROCKFORD, ILLINOIS

The Proper Gospel for

PALMARUM

And when they drew nigh unto Jerusalem, and were come to Bethphage, unto the mount of Olives, then sent Jesus two disciples, saying unto them, Go into the village over against you, and straightway ye shall find an ass tied, and a colt with her: loose them, and bring them unto me. And if any man say ought unto you, ye shall say, The Lord hath need of them; and straightway he will send them. All this was done, that it might be fulfilled which was spoken by the prophet, saying, Tell ye the daughter of Sion, Behold, thy King cometh unto thee, meek, and sitting upon an ass, and a colt the foal of an ass. And the disciples went, and did as Jesus commanded them, and brought the ass, and the colt, and put on them their clothes, and they set him thereon. And a very great multitude spread their garments in the way; others cut down branches from the trees, and strawed them in the way. And the multitudes that went before, and that followed, cried, saying, Hosanna to the son of David: Blessed is he that cometh in the name of the Lord; Hosanna in the highest.

—MATTHEW 21: 1-9.

THE HEART'S KING

PALM SUNDAY is a day of joy to all Christians. An irresistible joy thrusts out any thought or foreboding of the sad days just ahead. Real Christian joy has no darkening shadows. It was a day of victory, the triumph of it to reach through eternity.

This day was in the eternal plan of God. The prophet of old was pressed to say, "Rejoice greatly, O daughter of Zion; shout, O daughter of Jerusalem: behold, thy King cometh unto thee: he is just, and having salvation; lowly, and riding upon an ass, and upon a colt the foal of an ass."

The day of the fulfillment of this prophecy of Holy Writ had come. The Gospel story told so briefly, so simply, so reasonably and so sensibly reveals Divine inspiration.

What is the purpose of the story, we ask ourselves, and immediately we are led into deep meditation. The day as planned by the Master came as quietly and as irresistibly as the coming of the morning. It was not for His glory. He sought no glory who came to be born in a manger. It was that His glory might be revealed to the redeemed of earth,—that they might see their "heart's King" in His kingly simplicity and eternal glory.

The unpremeditated rejoicing of this day stirs us. Yet much of life's real joy is definitely unpremeditated, and often never anticipated. The Master's simple request to seek and to unloose the ass was soon fulfilled. Those near marveled no doubt at the full and quick completion of the disciples' errand. The apparent unprompted outburst of rejoicing must continue to engage the earnest thought of Christians down through the centuries. Who can understand it all? When we shall know one day the full meaning of this day possibly we shall know that something of the ecstasy of the day of Pentecost was upon the people. Is such a transport of real joy, and such an exuberant emotion beyond the dignity of Christians, or beyond the possibility for Christians? The world needs joy and emotion based upon eternal truth.

Perhaps for a brief moment the curtain of earth was withdrawn and the people got a momentary vision of the Saviour of mankind, or, perhaps, like another occasion "He opened their understanding." It may well have been another revelation of God as sure and definite as that revealed to the prophets of old. In such an hour an untutored people led, impromptu, by the joy of the day gave unqualified devotion to the Master, "Hosanna to the Son of David: Blessed is he that cometh in the name of the Lord." It was another evidence of the fulfillment of the prophecy of old. Who can devoutly study prophecy of the coming of the Christ without coming to an outburst

of joy such as this of the long ago? Surely God intended,
that as His prophets praised the coming of the Messiah,
so surely would the human voice give glorious testimony
to His appearance, unprompted by any plan or thought
of man, "Hosanna to the Son of David."

A King indeed! Not of an earthly crumbling kingdom; not in the tinseled splendor of an earthly king!
Meek indeed! The King of the heart. The King of a
kingdom—in this world, too, but not of it—but a King
of the realm eternal. The King of the redeemed of earth.
Who can measure the eternal joy of the souls redeemed—
the children of the great King.

The joyous company went on their joyous journey, a
journey all too short to Jerusalem. The rejoicing did not
lag. How could it in the presence of the King! We do
not know all the details—perhaps some fleet-footed runner
"caught up" in the spirit of the day looked for no greater
joy in life than to run on to Jerusalem to tell the gathering
multitude, "Behold thy King cometh." It must have been
something like that for in the Gospel of St. John we are
told, ". . . much people that were come to the feast, when
they heard that Jesus was coming to Jerusalem, took
branches of palm trees, and went forth to meet him, and
cried, Hosanna: Blessed is the King of Israel that cometh
in the name of the Lord." It was no small company apparently. A modern translator* has it, ". . . the great mass

---

* Moffatt

of people who had come up for the festival heard that Jesus was entering Jerusalem, and taking palm branches they went out to meet him, shouting, Hosanna! Blessed be he who comes in the Lord's name, the King of Israel!"

Undoubtedly the joyous procession increased as it made its way. People looked out of their doorways to see the strange procession. Others came out to ask, "Who is this?" Excited people could easily have hurled back the answer, "Listen to the shouting and you will know." Another earnest soul taking time reverently to answer, "This is the King of Israel," not knowing the full intent of his words.

The joyous company went on to the Temple. There were those, too, who recognized Jesus, and hated Him. There were those envious. Some find it so hard to see another honored. The soldier, sent by a government hostile to the Jew, was thinking in terms of order, and peace, and of the possibility of having to put down an insurrection. The skeptic standing by, hearing the multitude and the shouting of unalloyed joy, turned to sneer at the vagaries of simple people. It was all so simple—there was no marshall of the day. But the watching company apparently stepped aside as men do to make way for those who know where they are going. "Blessed is he that cometh in the name of the Lord." It is of the Lord that the multitude should take up the words of a prophetic Psalm of David. That gives an added authority to the

record of this day, and it is significant. He came to bless
all who "believe on his name." Who can bestow blessing
but He who is truly blessed? "This is my beloved Son, in
whom I am well pleased." The Master heard and saw the
manifestations of the love of those about Him. That is
never lost on the Master—but His thought went out to
the doubter, the skeptic, the sinner, the unsaved for whom
there was so little hope because of their hardness of heart.
Jesus would be the King of every heart.

He came in the "name of the Lord." Never an earthly
king came like that—or with so much authority. He was
soon to say that "All power is given unto me in heaven
and in earth." We give respect and honor, yea, place and
a hearing to one who comes in the name of our beloved
country, or in the name of the Church. A certain grandeur
fixes itself upon one sent on a great mission and going in
a great name. Jesus came in the Name of the Lord. Who
are we then that we should withhold the deepest devotion,
the most ardent love, and the fullest faith in our Redeemer? Our worship of Him today should be expressive
of the highest divinity in a redeemed human heart.

Jesus came to the Temple of the Lord. The Temple
was a symbol of the heart of Israel. Out of it should come
Israel's most transcendent hope, Israel's deep comfort and
joy. It was the House of Prayer for all peoples. But the
Temple like the heart of man was polluted. A strange
paradox! The clean rejoicing and hosannas terminated at

the Temple. There were worldliness, ungodliness, greed, selfishness, envy—the gamut of sin. What diligence and grace is needed to keep life clean and pure!

Jesus went into the Temple and "looked round about upon all things." What evident need of a Saviour! He had not come too soon. The cleansing power must begin. On this joyous Palm Sunday may the Lord as He comes to our hearts find them clean and joyous in singing, "Hosanna! Blessed is he that cometh in the name of the Lord." May He find that He is indeed the King of our heart.

As the last note of rejoicing fades with the shadows of evening there is a beautiful retrospect of Palm Sunday. John's Gospel records as the multitude shouted and recalled the prophecy, "Behold, thy King cometh, sitting on an ass's colt"—that, "These things understood not his disciples at the first: but when Jesus was glorified, then remembered they that these things were written of him, and that they had done these things unto him."

There must have been a reverent joy in their hearts as they thought of the real significance of this day and their witnessing of their Master. May the retrospect of this Palm Sunday give us the eternal joy that we, too, "had done these things unto him."

Monday in Holy Week

TO HIM BE GLORY!

HERBERT E. SCHILDROTH

Bethel Church
DETROIT, MICHIGAN

The Proper Gospel for

MONDAY IN HOLY WEEK

Then Jesus six days before the passover came to Bethany, where Lazarus was which had been dead, whom he raised from the dead. There they made him a supper; and Martha served: but Lazarus was one of them that sat at the table with him. Then took Mary a pound of ointment of spikenard, very costly, and anointed the feet of Jesus, and wiped his feet with her hair: and the house was filled with the odour of the ointment. Then saith one of his disciples, Judas Iscariot, Simon's son, which should betray him, Why was not this ointment sold for three hundred pence, and given to the poor? This he said, not that he cared for the poor; but because he was a thief, and had the bag, and bare what was put therein. Then said Jesus, Let her alone: against the day of my burying hath she kept this. For the poor always ye have with you; but me ye have not always. . . .

On the next day much people that were come to the feast, when they heard that Jesus was coming to Jerusalem, took branches of palm trees, and went forth to meet him, and cried, Hosanna: Blessed is the King of Israel that cometh in the name of the Lord. And Jesus, when he had found a young ass, sat thereon; as it is written, Fear not, daughter of Sion: behold, thy King cometh, sitting on an ass's colt. These things understood not his disciples at the first: but when Jesus was glorified, then remembered they that these things were written of him, and that they had done these things unto him. The people therefore that was with him when he called Lazarus out of his grave, and raised him from the dead, bare record. For this cause the people also met him, for that they heard that he had done this miracle. The Pharisees therefore said among themselves, Perceive ye how ye prevail nothing? behold, the world is gone after him. And there were certain Greeks among them that came up to worship at the feast: the same came therefore to Philip, which was of Bethsaida of Galilee, and desired him, saying, Sir, we would see Jesus. Philip cometh and telleth Andrew: and again Andrew and Philip tell Jesus. And Jesus answered them, saying, The hour is come, that the Son of man should be glorified.—JOHN 12: 1-23.

TO HIM BE GLORY!

TO desire glory is one of man's very common weaknesses. To give praise and honor to those to whom it is due is quite a general faculty with many. To try to prevent proper honors from being given those who merit the same, is the meanness of character in some. To discern the true picture in every case and to know something at least of real honor, real glory, is the qualification of those only who are in the fellowship of Christ in the fullest sense.

To him who is our very dear friend, we are usually willing and ready to give our heartiest felicitations, our sincerest greetings. Yes, we will go to great length to show our appreciation for his friendship, and manifest to the world that we recognize his attainments. But should it be so that we have some personal grievance against someone, it matters not how great a hero he may be, we will find reason, or excuse, to criticize, undermine, and, perhaps, go so far as to speak infamously about him in order to lower the estimate others may have of him.

Then, too, there is the question of what constitutes real honor, real glory. Some feel that to show their feelings for another they must exhibit a form of gushing over-statement. Others will go to great length to lavish with materialistic festivity. Some feel that the practices of an imperialistic or hierarchical politic are essential. Others are satisfied simply to look wide-eyed with mouth open in awe and amazement.

To follow Jesus on His road of suffering, to His death, and see Him rise again and ascend to the right hand of the Father, is to obtain the true understanding of honor, of glory and its bestowal and enjoyment. In our text we have several examples of attitudes expressing feelings relative to honor and glory. It is only after these have been exhausted and found wanting that we are led to look above the worldly practices and find the answer to the great question.

The Son of Man Should Be Glorified

To obtain the best possible understanding and application of this theme, we shall study the individual scenes of our text.

1. *In Humble Service*
2. *In Simple Faith*
3. *In Royal Allegiance*
4. *In Honest Quest*

1. *The Son of Man Should Be Glorified in Humble Service*

To the casual traveler, the village of Bethany would

be considered but a suburb of the more glorious city of Jerusalem. To Jesus it constituted a haven of rest and quiet on many an occasion. This village meant much to Him. In an humble home in this otherwise insignificant place, Jesus was always welcome. The people of this home were His friends and He was one to Whom they owed much. For had He not raised the brother from the dead? Had He not been in this home oft when the rest of the world had shown bitterness? He had said, "The foxes have holes and the birds have their nests, but the Son of man hath not where to lay his head." Although He had no such place by right of legal ownership, as the world demands, yet He was so loved in this home that it was always at His disposal. The scenes of our text begin in this home.

The Passover Feast was nigh. All the faithful would make their way to Jerusalem. Jesus and His disciples would go to the Holy City. But the hospitality of that city was known to Jesus. Had its king not tried to slay Him at the time of His birth? Had He not often met with disfavor in the theological circles of this center of religion? So in the season of approach to the Passover He spent time at Bethany, in the home of His friend Lazarus. No matter how welcome He was; no matter how often He came; He was always the guest of honor. Martha became busy and served a supper for Him. Lazarus was present. His disciples were with Him.

While they all partook of the supper prepared by Martha's hurried, yet humble service, Mary, who had sat at His feet ready to learn, and who had prepared especially for this very hour, took occasion to perform her humble service. Jesus and His disciples had journeyed afoot. It was customary to offer the guest a basin of water to refresh the weary feet, yes, even to bathe them for the tired traveler. While the others were busy with the meal, Mary carefully took her box of precious ointment and in a quiet fashion applied it to the feet of her beloved Master. In the deepest of humility, she then wiped His feet with her hair. Her "crowning glory" was not the center of attraction for her. At the very feet of Jesus, she would place her head. His was all the honor and all the glory in her heart and mind, in her whole life.

No one had paid any attention to Mary, nor to her service, nor to her box of ointment. But that ointment wasn't cheap. It had cost her something. It was "very costly." Not until the odor of the ointment had filled the room, and, therefore, could be noted and valued by the sense of smell, did anyone, other than Jesus, make any comment. And who should be the challenger? None other than the betrayer. His tender nostrils were trained to value odors. Priceless odors meant to him the expenditure of the currency of his day. In his own clever and deceitful manner, he let his character be known. Hiding behind the needs of the poor, he questioned the judgment of Jesus for permitting this humble service of Mary. What a contrast between the two, Mary and Judas. With Mary, Jesus was the one to be honored by a humble service. To Judas, this humble service, even for one so great as Jesus, was waste and misapplication of values.

Jesus settled the question. In His few terse statements to Judas, He has given a challenge to all who would know how to render true service and to discern true values. Mary had shown her feeling and her faith in her work. This humble service was given while Jesus was yet with her. Jesus would remind us that since He has physically left this world, we can still anoint Him by our ministry to the poor. That ointment was a preparation for His burial. Our ministry to the poor is an evidence that He still lives and the values of precious ointment are really measured by Him as they are ministered in humble service to those who are tired, weary, and in need. Thus He made manifest that to Him belongs the glory and the honor.

The fine spirit of Mary still lives. Many there are who would quietly and humbly kneel at His feet and apply their ointment of service. But it is also true that there is always a Judas, yes, far too many who would classify as such, to criticize, to belittle, to injure. Follow the example of Mary, for the Son of Man must be glorified even in humble service.

2. *And the Son of Man Must Be Glorified in Simple Faith*

While this episode took place in the little home in Bethany, there were many people gathered about. Of course, these people had been making their way to Jerusalem to exercise their religion in the annual feast of the Passover. They held dear the release from the bondage of slavery in Egypt many centuries before. They were grateful to the Eternal God for His infinite love and mercy made manifest in that delivery. It was not too much for them to travel many miles to commemorate this great fact in the keeping of the Passover. And they knew their prophecies concerning the delivery from the bondage of sin which had been promised. So it was that they were expectant and alert for the coming of the promised Messiah, the Saviour. These people made the little journey out to Bethany from Jerusalem. They knew Jesus was there. They had heard much about Him. His person was the fulfillment of their expectations. Many of them, perhaps, had seen Him as He had journeyed through their villages. They wanted to see Him again.

But they wanted more. They had heard that He had raised Lazarus from the dead. This was so unusual. No one else had done so great a deed. Could they but see Lazarus, they would be better able to believe what they had heard. We shouldn't wonder that they were slow to believe the things they heard. Lepers were being cleansed, the blind made to see, the deaf could hear again, the lame walked, and the dumb had been made to speak. But here at Bethany, the greatest proof of all had been given that the promised Saviour was come to deliver them. It was here that this Jesus had raised one from the dead. They wanted to see Jesus, yes, but they also wanted to see this Lazarus whom He had raised from the dead. For to see him would be to see the very object of the power made manifest by this Jesus in the act of raising him from the dead. Their simple faith had brought them to Jerusalem for the Passover. That faith had taken them out to Bethany to see Jesus. That faith needed something that would be given if they could but see Lazarus.

All this was causing great concern to the leaders of that day. The chief priests were troubled. They knew that the faith of many was growing. They knew that Lazarus' rising from the dead was a great aid to that faith in Jesus. They knew that if this movement should continue, their security in their offices would be shaken. How should they overcome? Why, simply kill Lazarus. Have him put out of the way. For, because of Lazarus, many of their people were following after Jesus and believing on Him.

The Passover Feast was supposed to be the center of attraction here. People, in simple faith, had come many miles to keep that feast. But the great problem for the leaders was that there was a faith just as simple, growing in power, which was being placed in the Son of Man who had come that whosoever would believe in Him should not perish but have everlasting life. We need this simple faith in the Son of Man today. Too much confidence is being placed in the things of the world, in political bosses, in "horses and chariots." Heroes are arising daily, and they receive the acclaim of the millions. But "the hour is come when the Son of Man should be glorified." And we know that in simple faith in Him we shake the powers of darkness and cause Satan's forces to tremble.

3. The Son of Man Should Be Glorified in Royal Allegiance

On the following day, Jesus and His disciples make their way to Jerusalem from Bethany. It was not long until the great throngs of faithful, gathered there, heard that He was about to enter the city. Practically, with one accord, they went out to meet Him. They took palm branches and joined the procession. The palm branch is symbolic of many things, principally signifying the head or chief of a group and great joy. Both of these applications stand out in this instance. For as Jesus rode ahead of the multitude, they expressed their great joy and gladness in Him, singing the Hosanna which declared Him to be their King. In this moment of great exultation, they gave to Him their allegiance. They placed their palms in the road that He might ride over them. They were His loyal subjects. His disciples did not understand. The people in the procession simply lived out the desire of their hearts. He was their King. They were His subjects, loyal and true, joyful and blessed, for this day their King had come in the Name of the Lord. The Son of Man should be glorified in joyful, royal allegiance. Again, the leaders of the Jews were touched with what was taking place. They saw their prestige waning. To them, He was drawing the world after Him. Something must be done. Their influence over the people was lost.

This is true today. When men and women are ready to glorify the Son of Man with their joyful and royal allegiance, the world stands in awe; the leaders quake, for they see their powers shaken. They try every means to overthrow this healthy relationship to Christ. But in their attempts, they only serve to increase the power and dominion of the Son of Man. Behold the nations where it has been tried.

4. *The Son of Man Should Be Glorified in Honest Quest*

Among the hosts in the city for the feast of the Passover, were Greeks who also had come to keep the feast. Their simple statement is a tremendous revelation. To Philip they simply said: "Sir, we would see Jesus!" That Jesus' own people should go after Him, does not seem so great a marvel. Here are aliens, foreigners, men of a different race. They are looking for Jesus. This amazed Philip. He told Andrew about it. And they are so thrilled, that they both carry the news to Jesus. His fame had spread. Men everywhere were now turning their attention to Him. He had become a world figure. But even though He was the center of conversation and debate among men, His was to be still something of a political matter. The attention which had become focused upon Him, would not easily be satisfied. Jesus realized this. And so it is that He answers Philip and Andrew with the statement that the "hour is come, that the Son of man should be glorified." In the honest quest of the Greeks, He had been given glory. When we present our Christ to the world in such a way that men and women and children come in search of further evidence of His love, and grace and mercy, in honest quest, it is a glory to our Christ.

But do we understand fully? The fullest glory came to Jesus, not through the humble service of Martha and Mary; not through simple faith of those who followed Him to Bethany; not through the royal allegiance shown during His triumphal procession; not through the honest quest of the Greeks; but four days later. It was then that the Son of Man fully came to be glorified. For when defeat on the Cross and in the grave was the pride of His opponents, Glory was His end and goal. That glory was consummated in His Resurrection and Ascension.

Today we wonder at the crossing of feelings as He, in our text, stood so close to His final hour in this world. But our understanding and appreciation of this text reaches its highest summit as we catch the full significance of His last statement: "The Son of man should be glorified." His glory sheds its light now upon all His work, sufferings, death, and resurrection, and we pray that we may glorify Him in humble service, in simple faith, in royal allegiance and in honest quest. Thus as these scenes of our text were later culminated by His being lifted up upon the Cross for the redemption of the world, so may He be lifted up in our hearts that His glory may brighten our lives and through us, the lives of others. "The hour is come, that the Son of man should be glorified." Amen.

Tuesday in Holy Week

LIFTED UP AND LIFTING ALL

FRED J. FIEDLER

Pastor, The Inner Mission
READING, PENNSYLVANIA

The Proper Gospel for

TUESDAY IN HOLY WEEK

Verily, verily, I say unto you, Except a corn of wheat fall into the ground and die, it abideth alone: but if it die, it bringeth forth much fruit. He that loveth his life shall lose it; and he that hateth his life in this world shall keep it unto life eternal. If any man serve me, let him follow me; and where I am, there shall also my servant be, if any man serve me, him will my Father honour. Now is my soul troubled; and what shall I say? Father, save me from this hour: but for this cause came I unto this hour. Father, glorify thy name. Then came there a voice from heaven, saying, I have both glorified it, and will glorify it again. The people therefore, that stood by, and heard it, said that it thundered: others said, An angel spake to him. Jesus answered and said, This voice came not because of me, but for your sakes. Now is the judgment of this world: now shall the prince of this world be cast out. And I, if I be lifted up from the earth, will draw all men unto me.

This he said, signifying what death he should die.

The people answered him, We have heard out of the law that Christ abideth for ever: and how sayest thou, The Son of man must be lifted up? who is this Son of man?

Then Jesus said unto them, Yet a little while is the light with you. Walk while ye have the light, lest darkness come upon you: for he that walketh in darkness knoweth not whither he goeth. While ye have light, believe in the light, that ye may be the children of light. These things spake Jesus, and departed, and did hide himself from them.

But though he had done so many miracles before them, yet they believed not on him. . . .

Nevertheless among the chief rulers also many believed on him; but because of the Pharisees they did not confess him, lest they should be put out of the synagogue: for they loved the praise of men more than the praise of God.—JOHN 12: 24-43.

LIFTED UP AND LIFTING ALL

I, if I be lifted up will draw all men unto me.—JOHN 12: 32.

IT is very thrilling to see how this word of Jesus has been fulfilled. Lifted up on the cross He has indeed been drawing all men unto Him. The poor and the lowly have been drawn to Him. Those who live in kings' houses have responded to His power to draw men to Him. Many have come from the north and the south and the east and the west and they have taken their places in the Kingdom of God. They have been drawn by the Christ who died for them on the cross.

Right there on the hill of Calvary we see the great movement to Jesus begin. Drawn to Jesus Christ first of all was a bad man, the penitent thief on the cross. Deep within him was a strong human urge to find a worthy object of allegiance, which, reaching out at that last moment, found Jesus. But there was not only a repentant sinner, drawn to Jesus in the hour of death. There was also a leader of men, a Roman officer, who beheld the suffering of Christ and listened to His last words, and said at the end of it: "Surely this was a righteous man; surely this was the Son of God." And we have the sacred record telling us that many people who came out to see the crucifixion, "beholding the things which were done, smote their breasts and returned to the city."

Within the same year thousands of people who listened to the testimony of the apostles were drawn to Jesus and became followers of the Way. They were drawn by the Christ who was lifted up on the cross; for we know from their own assertions that the apostles faithfully and steadfastly preached "Christ and him crucified." And so we trace that message of the crucified Christ as it followed the civilized highways of the Roman Empire, and then penetrated the trackless wilderness of northern and western Europe, and again and again we count the multitudes drawn to Him who was lifted up on the cross.

In our own day the message is still proclaimed to the far ends of the earth. Just a few years ago a well-known journalist was sent by a famous American publisher to travel in the Orient with the special purpose of finding out just what the Christian Gospel was doing for the world. That journalist visited dozens of Christian missionary establishments and came back home thoroughly converted to the great missionary work of the Church. And as to the Christ of the Cross, this is what he said: "Wherever I went I always asked people the question:

'In all the Christian message what was the one part more than any other which caused you to become Christian?' And ever and always the answer was, 'The story of the Cross'."

So there you have it. This holy week in which we review again the tragic hours of Gethsemane and Calvary, we give glory to God that we may know of a certainty the fulfillment of the words of Jesus: "I, if I be lifted up, will draw all men unto me."

In relation to this great prophecy of Jesus we hear Him saying something about sacrifice in terms of the grain of wheat which is planted in the soil, and we hear Him call those who serve Him to follow Him, and we hear Him give His warning to those who refuse to follow the light.

I.   "Except a grain of wheat fall into the ground and die it abideth alone, but if it die it bringeth forth much fruit." Here is Jesus' declaration of sacrifice. His death on the cross is the sacrifice which brings hope and life to men. A grain of wheat cast into the ground dies as a grain of wheat. But something wonderful happens. New life comes forth and that new life is multiplied many-fold and it gives life to men. But it must die first, for if it is not cast into the ground to die it continues lifeless. It is just another grain of wheat and remains only that. Indeed we remember how Jesus, living among men, was despised and rejected. With all His works of wonder and helpfulness He was still very much alone and even His own disciples had no real sense of His purpose. It was necessary for Him to die so that the living fruit of His sacrifice on the cross could be made to flourish among men, through the enlightenment of the Holy Spirit, bringing all things to their remembrance.

If Jesus had not gone to the cross of Calvary there could have been no pardon and peace of God filling the hearts of men, for without the shedding of blood there is no forgiveness of sins. If Jesus had not gone to the cross to die for us we would still be groping with Job and saying: "O, that I knew where I might find him." That universal human cry gathered up in the question of Job is answered on Calvary. There we behold the Lamb of God which taketh away the sin of the world. There we hear the final words of Jesus, "It is finished," and we see the glory of God accomplished in the redemption of the world.

And Jesus has made plain to us that His sacrifice is not only our hope but it is also a pattern for us. "He that loveth his life shall lose it and he that hateth his life for my sake shall keep it unto life eternal." And that means that if we live only for ourselves, our lives are confined to the material things of life and they come to an end with death. But if we keep the material things of life in their proper subordinate place, while we cultivate the inner life and seek to grow in spirit, we shall have something that still goes on with us beyond the grave to eternal habitations. And not only that, but if we give self-sacrifice its rightful place in our Christian lives we shall find happiness also here in this world through the happiness which we bring to others. And there is no joy that we can have which is so satisfying as that which comes to us when we are conscious that by our self-sacrificing lives we have awakened in others a living faith in Christ.

Here is the testimony of a man in a hospital room. In the other bed was a servant of God who with his good wife gave up many attractive things in the world for the sake of giving their substance and their lives to the work of making known to others the saving Gospel of Christ. The wife came every day to visit her sick husband and the man in the other bed at first paid little attention to them. But now and then he caught the outline of a story unmistakably human, but lighted up by a touch of the divine, a story of the power of God's Word changing human lives. It was the wife telling of the triumph of the Gospel in some wayward human life. Then too day after day in that sick room the wife read to her husband from the sacred pages of God's Word and at the end of it she bowed her head in quiet unaffected prayer.

This is the testimony of the man in the other bed in that semi-private room: "I never had much belief in anything and never bothered with the Church, but when I gradually listened more and more to those two devoted people, I discovered that they had something which I did not have. It was something which meant a great deal to them and it was real to them. I decided that now I could see something in the Christian faith that I never saw before. I asked them if I could have part in their daily devotions. Now I have been baptized and I am learning to find a joy in life that I never knew before. It is the joy of having something to do with the One who was lifted up on the cross for me."

II.   Here is also Jesus' call to serve and follow Him. "If any man serve me let him follow me." For many people it seems very light and easy to serve Christ. Perhaps it is light and easy because they follow Him only afar off. In our luxury-loving age how seldom it occurs to people actually to deny themselves something for the sake of following Christ in any true sense. In our age of ease and comfort how much do people think of accepting real hardship as a manifestation of loyalty to the Way of Christ? And this is a legitimate inquiry, for here is Jesus telling about the trouble of His soul as He thinks of the suffering that He has to face and endure. "Shall I ask the Father to deliver me from this time of suffering?" He asks. "No, that is impossible, for this is my purpose in the world—to go through this suffering." And then he receives the promise that God's Name will be glorified through His suffering. And that is why we can talk of the glory of the cross. Through suffering on the cross our sins are atoned for. We glorify God for His great gift of salvation by the cross.

History gives us examples of the followers of Jesus going through suffering for His sake. Courageous thousands have endured persecution and death to follow Christ. One well-known expression has the sound of a proverb and it tells much of the suffering of Christ's followers: "The blood of the martyrs is the seed of the Church." In our own modern day we have heard something of the suffering of Christian ministers in Europe, brave men who refuse to have any supreme leader except Jesus Christ alone. Our hearts have been thrilled by the open declaration of the Lutheran ministers of Norway who chose the way of suffering with unbroken faithfulness to their Lord, rather than the favor of a tyrant through treason to Christ.

For the last several years we have been hearing how the Chinese people have changed their attitude toward Christians and missionaries. It is because of what the missionaries endured in the Japanese invasion since 1937. Many people from Europe and America, engaged in business and industry in China, left the country and returned home to escape the dangers of invasion and war and destruction. But the Christian missionaries remained in China, sharing the sufferings of their Chinese brethren, taking care of the sick and wounded, opening relief stations for the hungry and needy. Again and again when they were asked to avoid dangers and return home, they refused, saying they were needed more than ever to help a suffering people.

The people of China said: "If the Christian Gospel makes people do what these Christian missionaries have been doing, then we want that Christian Gospel." So missionaries have been invited and welcomed into interior China because government and people alike recognize in them the spirit which will save a country and its people. "If any man serve me let him follow me." These servants of Christ in a foreign land have followed in very truth. They followed the Way of Christ and their serving and their following have won the love of a great nation, and they have obtained an open door for Christ our Saviour.

But we ask ourselves how much we should be willing to endure as followers of Jesus Christ. There are some brave souls who endure the displeasure of some members of their own families because they are faithful members of the Church. They serve Christ and to do so they follow Him through suffering. Here is a group of men in prison who respond to the call for Bible class and who do so in spite of the jibes and sneers and mockery of some of their fellow prisoners. We can find the courage of the martyr in some humble places. But there are those who will not endure giving up any of the various pleasures of the world in order to take part in Christ's program for the saving of the world. We need to ask ourselves: "How much are *we* willing to go through for the sake of being followers of Christ our Saviour?" Indeed we need to do more than ask ourselves that question. We need to make our faith in Christ alive by going where He has gone—into the experience of self-denial and self-sacrifice, that we may humble ourselves and give glory to Him who was lifted up on the cross for our sakes.

III.   But here also is Jesus' warning to those who refuse to see the light and follow it. "Walk while ye have the light lest darkness come upon you." It was the answer of Jesus to those who expressed their doubts about Him. That the Son of Man should be lifted up on the cross— this was hard for them to believe. They had their own ideas about how the Messiah should come to rule in earthly glory among them. And yet they had the prophets. They had the Scriptures. They had the doctors and teachers. And here was Jesus living among them, the certain fulfillment of all the words of the prophets. Here was the Light among them but they would not give heed to the Light. They would not follow Him.

It is a tragic mistake to be heedless of the light. In the story of Dives and Lazarus, you remember, the man who did not walk in the light while he lived on earth, begged that someone might go back from the dead to warn his brothers lest they come to the same place of torment. But the answer was, "They have Moses and the prophets; if they will not hear them, neither will they listen though one came back from the dead." We cannot help but think of the vast amount of unbelief all around us. Among our friends, among the people with whom we work, sometimes even in our own families, unbelief raises its unruly voice and tries to appear brave by being loud and assertive, like the small boy who whistles to keep up his courage while he is going through some dark place.

Indifference to Christ and to His Church and to His way of life is simply the result of unbelief. We call it darkness and certainly many dark deeds are done where there is no belief in God. But here in the Gospel is the light which can dispel the darkness of unbelief and make glad every human heart that discovers hope and the promise of abundant life in Him who has called Himself the Light of the world. And the value of the light which we have in Christ is manifest in the good works—the fruits of those lives which walk by that Light.

Tragic indeed is the human stubbornness which refuses to heed the light. It is a common thing to say that we all must die. True as it is we have a way of avoiding the thought of death. Yet it is bound to come and each one of us has to face it by himself. Many people are well prepared for death. They have arranged for their property and they have designated who is to have what is left. They have specified what kind of a coffin and how deep a grave. They have carried the proper life insurance. But too many have not made the one most necessary preparation for death and that is to walk in the Light while they live. To walk with Christ here in this life so that we may know Him and He may know us in the life beyond—that is the most essential preparation for death, and Jesus here gives His admonition to believe in the Light that we may be children of light.

As children of light we go with Jesus through this holy week and bow before Him in worship and in prayer. God grant that we may be drawn to Him and that we may gather His Word into our very hearts and understand all that He has accomplished for us by His sacrifice on the cross. As children of light we must get for ourselves the faith and the courage to serve Him with whatever talents we possess and to follow Him with devotion and self-denial. God grant that our devotion and self-denial may always be of that sincere kind which makes us sure, and makes others sure, that we really mean it when we say we are followers of Jesus Christ. He has drawn us to Him because He was lifted up on the cross. As children of the light we can help to overcome the unbelief of the world. Let us add our faithful witness of Christ our Saviour who was lifted up on the cross that He might draw all men unto Himself.

Wednesday in Holy Week
WHAT DO YOU WANT?

CHARLES A. LINN, PH.D., D.D.
Church of the Ascension
SAVANNAH, GEORGIA

The Proper Gospel for

WEDNESDAY IN HOLY WEEK

Now the feast of unleavened bread drew nigh, which is called the Passover. And the chief priests and scribes sought how they might kill him; for they feared the people.

Then entered Satan into Judas surnamed Iscariot, being of the number of the twelve. And he went his way, and communed with the chief priests and captains, how he might betray him unto them. And they were glad, and covenanted to give him money. And he promised, and sought opportunity to betray him unto them in the absence of the multitude.

Then came the day of unleavened bread, when the passover must be killed. And he sent Peter and John, saying, Go and prepare us the passover, that we may eat. And they said unto him, Where wilt thou that we prepare? And he said unto them, Behold, when ye are entered into the city, there shall a man meet you, bearing a pitcher of water; follow him into the house where he entereth in. And ye shall say unto the goodman of the house, The Master saith unto thee, Where is the guestchamber, where I shall eat the passover with my disciples? And he shall shew you a large upper room furnished: there make ready. And they went, and found as he had said unto them: and they made ready the passover.

And when the hour was come, he sat down, and the twelve apostles with him. And he said unto them, With desire I have desired to eat this passover with you before I suffer: for I say unto you, I will not any more eat thereof, until it be fulfilled in the kingdom of God.

And he took the cup, and gave thanks, and said, Take this, and divide it among yourselves: for I say unto you, I will not drink of the fruit of the vine, until the kingdom of God shall come.

And he took bread, and gave thanks, and brake it, and gave unto them, saying, This is my body which is given for you: this do in remembrance of me. Likewise also the cup after supper, saying, This cup is the new testament in my blood, which is shed for you. But, behold, the hand of him that betrayeth me is with me on the table. And truly the Son of man goeth, as it was determinded: but woe unto that man by whom he is betrayed! And they began to enquire among themselves, which of them it was that should do this thing.

And there was also a strife among them, which of them should be accounted the greatest. And he said unto them, The kings of the Gentiles exercise lordship over them; and they that exercise authority upon them are called benefactors. But ye shall not be so: but he that is greatest among you, let him be as the younger; and he that is chief, as he that doth serve. For whether is greater, he that sitteth at meat, or he that serveth? is not he that sitteth at meat? but I am among you as he that serveth. Ye are they which have continued with me in my temptations. And I appoint unto you a kingdom, as my Father hath appointed unto me; that ye may eat and drink at my table in my kingdom, and sit on thrones judging the twelve tribes of Israel.

And the Lord said, Simon, Simon, behold, Satan hath desired to have you, that he may sift you as wheat: but I have prayed for thee, that thy faith fail not: and when thou art converted, strengthen thy brethren. And he said unto him, Lord, I am ready to go with thee, both into prison, and to death. And he said, I tell thee, Peter, the cock shall not crow this day, before that thou shalt thrice deny that thou knowest me. And he said unto them, When I sent you without purse, and scrip, and shoes, lacked ye any thing? And they said, Nothing. Then said he unto them, But now, he that hath a purse, let him take it, and likewise his scrip: and he that hath no sword, let him sell his garment, and buy one. For I say unto you, that this that is written must yet be accomplished in me, And he was reckoned among the transgressors: for the things concerning me have an end. And they said, Lord, behold, here are two swords. And he said unto them, It is enough.

And he came out, and went, as he was wont, to the mount of Olives; and his disciples also followed him. And when he was at the place, he said unto them, Pray that ye enter not into temptation. And he was withdrawn from them about a stone's cast, and kneeled down, and prayed, saying, Father, if thou be willing, remove this cup from me: nevertheless not my will, but thine, be done. And there appeared an angel unto him from heaven, strengthening him. And being in an agony he prayed more earnestly: and his sweat was as it were great drops of blood falling down to the ground. And when he rose up from prayer, and was come to his disciples, he found them sleeping for sorrow, and said unto them, Why sleep ye? rise and pray, lest ye enter into temptation.

And while he yet spake, behold a multitude, and he that was called Judas, one of the twelve, went before them, and drew near unto Jesus to kiss him. But Jesus said unto him, Judas, betrayest thou the Son of man with a kiss? When they which were about him saw what would follow, they said unto him, Lord, shall we smite with the sword? And one of them smote the servant of the high priest, and cut off his right ear. And Jesus answered and said, Suffer ye thus far. And he touched his ear, and healed him. Then Jesus said unto the chief priests, and captains of the temple, and the elders, which were come to him, Be ye come out, as against a thief, with swords and staves? When I was daily with you in the temple, ye stretched forth no hands against me: but this is your hour, and the power of darkness.

Then took they him, and led him, and brought him into the high priest's house. And Peter followed afar off. And when they had kindled a fire in the midst of the hall, and were set down together, Peter sat down among them. But a certain maid beheld him as he sat by the fire, and earnestly looked upon him, and said, This man was also with him. And he denied him, saying, Woman, I know him not. And after a little while another saw him, and said, Thou art also of them. And Peter said, Man, I am not. And about the space of one hour after another confidently affirmed, saying, Of a truth this fellow also was with him: for he is a Galilaean. And Peter said, Man, I know not what thou sayest. And immediately, while he yet spake, the cock crew. And the Lord turned, and looked upon Peter. And Peter remembered the word of the Lord, how he had said unto him, Before the cock crow, thou shalt deny me thrice. And Peter went out and wept bitterly.

And the men that held Jesus mocked him, and smote him. And when they had blindfolded him, they struck him on the face, and asked him, saying, Prophesy, who is it that smote thee? And many other things blasphemously spake they against him.

And as soon as it was day, the elders of the people and the chief priests and the scribes came together, and led him into their council, saying, Art thou the Christ? tell us. And he said unto them, If I tell you, ye will not believe: and if I also ask you, ye will not answer me, nor let me go. Hereafter shall the Son of man sit on the right hand of the power of God. Then said they all, Art thou then the Son of God? And he said unto them, Ye say that I am. And they said, What need we any further witness? for we ourselves have heard of his own mouth.

And the whole multitude of them arose, and led him unto Pilate. And they began to accuse him, saying, We found this fellow perverting the nation, and forbidding to give tribute to Caesar, saying that he himself is Christ a King. And Pilate asked him, saying, Art thou the King of the Jews? And he answered him and said, Thou sayest it. Then said Pilate to the chief priests and to the people, I find no fault in this man. And they were the more fierce, saying, He stirreth up the people, teaching throughout all Jewry, beginning from Galilee to this place. When Pilate heard of Galilee, he asked whether the man were a Galilaean. And as soon as he knew that he belonged unto Herod's jurisdiction, he sent him to Herod, who himself also was at Jerusalem at that time.

And when Herod saw Jesus, he was exceeding glad: for he was desirous to see him of a long season, because he had heard many things of him; and he hoped to have seen some miracle done by him. Then he questioned with him in many words; but he answered him nothing. And the chief priests and scribes stood and vehemently accused him. And Herod with his men of war set him at nought, and mocked him, and arrayed him in a gorgeous robe, and sent him again to Pilate. And the same day

Pilate and Herod were made friends together: for before they were at enmity between themselves.

And Pilate, when he had called together the chief priests and the rulers and the people, said unto them, Ye have brought this man unto me, as one that perverteth the people: and behold, I, having examined him before you, have found no fault in this man touching those things whereof ye accuse him: no, nor yet Herod: for I sent you to him; and, lo, nothing worthy of death is done unto him. I will therefore chastise him, and release him. (For of necessity he must release one unto them at the feast.) And they cried out all at once, saying, Away with this man, and release unto us Barabbas: (who for a certain sedition made in the city, and for murder, was cast into prison.) Pilate therefore, willing to release Jesus, spake again to them. But they cried, saying, Crucify him, crucify him. And he said unto them the third time, Why, what evil hath he done? I have found no cause of death in him: I will therefore chastise him, and let him go. And they were instant with loud voices, requiring that he might be crucified. And the voices of them and of the chief priests prevailed. And Pilate gave sentence that it should be as they required. And he released unto them him that for sedition and murder was cast into prison, whom they had desired; but he delivered Jesus to their will.

And as they led him away, they laid hold upon one Simon, a Cyrenian, coming out of the country, and on him they laid the cross, that he might bear it after Jesus.

And there followed him a great company of people, and of women, who also bewailed and lamented him. But Jesus turning unto them said, Daughters of Jerusalem, weep not for me, but weep for yourselves, and for your children. For, behold, the days are coming, in the which they shall say, Blessed are the barren, and the wombs that never bare, and the paps which never gave suck. Then shall they begin to say to the mountains, Fall on us; and to the hills, Cover us. For if they do these things in a green tree, what shall be done in the dry?

And there were also two other, malefactors, led with him to be put to death. And when they were come to the place, which is called Calvary, there they crucified him, and the malefactors, one on the right hand, and the other on the left.

Then said Jesus, Father, forgive them; for they know not what they do. And they parted his raiment, and cast lots. And the people stood beholding. And the rulers also with them derided him, saying, He saved others; let him save himself, if he be Christ, the chosen of God. And the soldiers also mocked him, coming to him, and offering him vinegar, and saying, If thou be the king of the Jews, save thyself.

And a superscription also was written over him in letters of Greek, and Latin, and Hebrew, THIS IS THE KING OF THE JEWS.

And one of the malefactors which were hanged railed on him, saying, If thou be Christ, save thyself and us. But the other answering rebuked him, saying, Dost not thou fear God, seeing thou art in the same condemnation? And we indeed justly; for we receive the due reward of our deeds: but this man hath done nothing amiss. And he said unto Jesus, Lord, remember me when thou comest into thy kingdom. And Jesus said unto him, Verily I say unto thee, To day shalt thou be with me in paradise.

And it was about the sixth hour, and there was a darkness over all the earth until the ninth hour. And the sun was darkened, and the veil of the temple was rent in the midst.

And when Jesus had cried with a loud voice, he said, Father, into thy hands I commend my spirit: and having said thus, he gave up the ghost.

Now when the centurion saw what was done, he glorified God, saying, Certainly this was a righteous man. And all the people that came together to that sight, beholding the things which were done, smote their breasts, and returned. And all his acquaintance, and the women that followed him from Galilee, stood afar off, beholding these things.—LUKE 22: 1—23: 49.

WHAT DO YOU WANT?

With desire I have desired to eat this passover with you before I suffer.—LUKE 22: 15.

THE time is at hand when Jesus must be crucified. Upon His heart and soul is a heavy burden. It is not self-pity, arising from the injustice of impending condemnation. It is not fear, because of the agonies that He must endure. It is a deep desire that must be satisfied; a profound purpose, that cannot be turned aside. It is the one thing above all else that He wants.

Jesus clearly states His desire, and in the succeeding hours adequately amplifies it. How much easier would it be in this world to understand spiritual values, or even to transact the ordinary business of life, if the secret desire of men's hearts were known—if it were possible to have from every one a plain and simple answer to the question: "What do you want?"

A stranger knocks at my door. He is admitted and comfortably seated. He proves to be a fluent conversationalist as he talks about the weather, the war, and the will-o'-the-wisp. I prove to be a fair philosopher, as I speculate on the section of country from which he comes, the nationality of his ancestors, and more particularly on the question as to whether or not he is a book agent. All the while there is one burning question upon my mind. Were it not that the conventions of polite society forbid me to be rude, I should ask him point blank: "What do you want?"

A politician asks me to vote for him. He promises me to uphold the constitution, to clean up every vice "from Greenland's icy mountains to India's coral strand," and to get a new postoffice for my community. I'm not much interested in his promises, but I'd like to ask him: "What do you want? What is the basis of your one supreme desire to hold this office?"

A religious leader is dull or brilliant, halting or eloquent, timid or expressively dramatic. If I must appraise his value to the Christian cause, I must have an answer from the depths of his soul to my basic question: "What do you want? What is the motivation of your ministry?"

David's Confession

It may seem impertinent to ask such questions of our contemporaries. But the lives of the great characters of the Scripture are to us as open books. On the historian's magic carpet we may flit back across the centuries and ask what we like. Let's make an expedition to the royal palace of the great king of ancient Israel, and ask David: "What do you want? What is your supreme desire?" Immediately the answer comes back in the words of his prayer:

> "Create in me a clean heart, O God;
> And renew a right spirit within me."

No one understands life unless he recognizes the fact that the hidden stream from which it springs, whether pure or polluted, is desire. The Psalmist, in an hour of deep penitence, acknowledges his sins and transgressions. These represent to him predominantly the life that he has lived in the sphere of reality. But he discerns also the source from which this impure life has sprung. He does not try to shift the responsibility by placing the blame on his environment, but confesses the fault is within himself.

The evil desires of his heart are so deep-seated that he can explain them only as fundamental characteristics of the nature with which he came into the world. Conceived and born in sin, he has no power within himself to overcome the natural bent of his depraved will. Only God can wash away his sin, and blot out his inward iniquity. Only God can open his lips and fashion his life, that his every thought, word, and deed may be a credit to his creator.

The answer of the Psalmist presents a clear picture of human desire. By nature it is impure, and at enmity with God. By the grace and mercy of God it may be cleansed, and redirected into the ways of righteousness.

Jesus' Reply

Coming down across the centuries, into "the fullness of time," we meet Jesus. Not critically, but for the sake of His instructive example, we ask Him too: "What do you want? What is your deep desire?" In all simplicity He replies: "My meat is to do the will of him that sent me."

Jesus "was in all points tempted like as we are, yet without sin." In Him there is no lust that must be purged away. His desire, and the will of the Father, are one. If we follow Him from the time that He was about His Father's business in the Temple at the age of twelve, down to the end of His earthly ministry, we find both the essence and expression of His life an unceasing prayer: "Thy will be done."

Behold Him as He comes to the closing session of the greatest school that was ever conducted on earth, taught by Him who is Himself the Truth, not abstract, nor limited by the inadequate art of human language, but personal, vibrant with eternal reality, and articulate with divine authority. The school of the Apostles is tense, eagerly expectant, fearful in anticipation of the event which the Master has prophesied. Silence reigns as they listen for His opening words. Then He speaks: "With desire I have desired to eat this passover with you before I suffer."

The passover perpetuated the memory of the Children of Israel's deliverance from the bondage of Egypt. It was also a prophecy of the deliverance of all the children of God from the bondage of sin. The blood of the lamb sprinkled upon the doorposts and lintels in the land of Goshen had caused the angel of death to pass over every home of the Hebrew people. In like manner the blood of "the Lamb of God, which taketh away the sin of the world" is to spare from eternal death every human soul who puts his trust in the promises of God and their fulfillment in His beloved Son, Jesus Christ, the Saviour of the world.

It is the supreme desire of Jesus: in keeping with the eternal purpose and plan of His Father, to fulfill these promises; by His atoning sacrifice, to open the way of salvation; and through His divine instruction, to lay the groundwork of His Church, that throughout the ages to come He may truly be "a ransom for many."

"This passover," which He is about to eat with His disciples, is the last passover under the old covenant. The Paschal Lamb of the new covenant is about to be offered in sacrifice. Henceforth, when they keep the feast, the bread and the wine will be not merely symbols, but vehicles of His living Presence, the divine seal of their salvation.

In the institution of the Holy Supper Jesus wants them to know, and to have always before them the fact that their salvation depends, not alone upon His vicarious sacrifice, but also upon His living Presence with and in them. This indwelling of Christ is to bring about in them a complete change of personal attitudes. No longer are they to strive among themselves as to "which of them should be accounted the greatest." Dominated by Him as their Master, they must be, like Him, "as he that serveth." They must be ready to meet temptation and actual hostility on the part of their spiritual enemy. And they are to be ready like Him to lay down their lives for the cause of the Kingdom, with the same sure confidence of triumphant victory over death. And, unto the end, they are to be animated by the spirit of love, even toward their enemies and executioners.

The earnest desire with which Jesus seeks opportunity to eat this passover with His disciples is utterly devoid of self-seeking. He wants nothing for Himself, not even the preservation of His own life. He is still about His Father's business, and He does not want to end His life without being able to say: "It is finished."

Behind him is a life of voluntary humiliation. Before Him is the way of the Cross—and then the victory. Those who are gathered with Him in the upper room, to eat with Him this last passover, have been with Him during the years in which He has known hunger and weariness, and has had no place to lay His head. They have seen men come to Him in the sanctimonious attitude of saints, but with the sinister motive of trying to entrap Him in His speech. They had heard even the legions of hell cry out against Him. But they have known also the power of His Word, and the divinity of His person.

Now they are to see Him give Himself into the hands of His enemies, to be mocked and despitefully treated, and then to become "obedient unto death, even the death of the cross." The earnest desire of Jesus is that, though they may not understand the mysteries of this tragic hour, they may be prepared to await the unfolding of the bitter bud of His atoning sacrifice, into the sweet and beauteous flower of eternal salvation.

The Testimony of the Teeming Myriads

It is said that if the Chinese people marched four abreast, at army pace, the procession would never end, for the reason that their birth rate is greater than the rate at which this marching host would pass any given point. Translate this thought into a picture of the teeming myriads of all nations, marching down through two millenniums, and we shall have, so far as the human mind is able to grasp it, a conception of the enormous scope of human desire, which has made the life of the world since Jesus lived on earth.

Out of the world have come the desires of the flesh. Into the world, from the living Lord, have come the desires of the Spirit. The clash of these inward urges has produced a humanity which appears upon the surface to be a Dr. Jekyll and Mr. Hyde. Out of the desires of the

Spirit have developed magnanimous philanthropy, sympathetic humanitarianism, and all the list of Christian virtues. Out of the desires of the natural world have evolved lust and hatred and annihilating war. But by the powers of heaven and hell this Dr. Jekyll and Mr. Hyde is a different character. By nature a sordid soul, committed to the ways of concupiscence, he is slowly but surely being transformed, by the renewing of the Spirit, into the ways of eternal righteousness. In his effort to purify his soul he may have to cast off some of his members—cut off a hand perhaps, or pluck out an eye—but, by the grace of God, he will not cease to proceed in the direction of eternal and spiritual victory.

Ask the world, "What do you want?" and the answer is confusion. But hark! Out of the crowd comes a clear and ringing voice: "For me to live is Christ, and to die is gain." And behold! A holy band of saints, and martyrs, and apostles, led by the Son of God! In their bodies they bear the marks of battle "against principalities, against powers, against the rulers of the darkness of this world, against spiritual wickedness in high places." Above them waves a sacred banner, and in their voices is the sound of victory, as they sing:

> "In the Cross of Christ I glory,
>   Towering o'er the wrecks of time;
>   All the light of sacred story
>   Gathers round its head sublime."

The little band moves out and mingles with the crowd. Their banners and their songs are multiplied. Among them are few of the mighty men of this world. Their only weapon is a Book. But, oh, their faith!—their faith in this Book! and in the Lamb of God, Who lives and brings them, through this sacred Word, the blessings of salvation! Yes, their faith! for "this is the victory that overcometh the world."

Ours is the victory, too, through the "blood and sweat" of these men of God, who have kept pure the stream of living water, by which our hearts are cleansed, and a right Spirit is renewed within us. And ours is the faith triumphant. If someone turn and ask us, "What do you want?" let them hear our answer while we pray:

> "Anoint me with Thy heavenly grace,
>   Adopt me for thine own,
> That I may see Thy glorious face,
>   And worship at Thy throne.
>
> "Let every thought, and work, and word
>   To Thee be ever given:
> Then life shall be Thy service, Lord,
>   And death the gate of heaven."

Thursday in Holy Week

SERVICE—A GODSEND

ALVIN E. BELL, D.D.
Glenwood Church
TOLEDO, OHIO

The Proper Gospel for

THURSDAY IN HOLY WEEK

Now before the feast of the passover, when Jesus knew that his hour was come that he should depart out of this world unto the Father, having loved his own which were in the world, he loved them unto the end. And supper being ended, the devil having now put into the heart of Judas Iscariot, Simon's son, to betray him; Jesus knowing that the Father had given all things into his hands, and that he was come from God, and went to God; he riseth from supper, and laid aside his garments; and took a towel, and girded himself. After that he poureth water into a bason, and began to wash the disciples' feet, and to wipe them with the towel wherewith he was girded. Then cometh he to Simon Peter: and Peter saith unto him, Lord, dost thou wash my feet? Jesus answered and said unto him, What I do thou knowest not now; but thou shalt know hereafter. Peter saith unto him, Thou shalt never wash my feet. Jesus answered him, If I wash thee not, thou hast no part with me. Simon Peter saith unto him, Lord, not my feet only, but also my hands and my head. Jesus saith to him, He that is washed needeth not save to wash his feet, but is clean every whit: and ye are clean, but not all. For he knew who should betray him; therefore said he, Ye are not all clean. So after he had washed their feet, and had taken his garments, and was set down again, he said unto them, Know ye what I have done to you? Ye call me Master and Lord: and ye say well; for so I am. If I then, your Lord and Master, have washed your feet; ye also ought to wash one another's feet. For I have given you an example, that ye should do as I have done to you.—JOHN 13: 1-15.

SERVICE—A
GODSEND

For I have given you an example, that ye should do as I have done to you.—JOHN 13: 15 (JOHN 13: 1-15).

FORTY-FOUR times in the Gospel according to John our Lord Jesus speaks of Himself as a "Godsend" to the world. The last of these, in John 20: 21, is shaped in the identical mold in which our text is shaped: "As my Father hath sent me, even so send I you." He commends to us for the shaping of our lives this same mold in which His own was fashioned, when, in the verse immediately following our text and lesson He says, "Verily, verily, I say unto you, The servant is not greater than his lord: neither he that is sent greater than he that sent him." In His great high-priestly prayer in the upper room He prayed to His Father after the same manner, saying, "As thou hast sent me into the world, even so have I also sent them into the world." As He was the Father's "Godsend" to serve, so we, His disciples, are to be His "Godsends" to serve after the pattern of His example: "For I have given you an example, that ye should do as I have done to you."

Deep down in this conviction of His having been sent of God our Lord buttressed all of His service to His disciples and to the world: "Jesus knowing that the Father had given all things into his hands, and that he was come from God, and went to God; he riseth from supper, and laid aside his garments; and took a towel, and girded himself. After that he poureth water into a bason, and began to wash the disciples' feet, and to wipe them with the towel wherewith he was girded."

Far from regarding His heavenly origin as a ground for seeking exemption, or even deferment from service, it was to Him the very reason and ground for His compulsion to service, even of the most menial type. He did not regard His divine Sonship with the Father as ground for His seeking a "commission," enabling Him to give commands instead of serving in the ranks. There was no service so menial as to be inconsistent with His being sent from God and returning to God.

With the mud and manure of the streets upon their sandals and making uncomfortable, if not ill-smelling, their feet and their Master's, every last one of the Twelve knew that the most urgent service waiting to be performed was that of removing those sandals and washing their feet of the filth of the streets through which they had just walked. Indeed, the goodman of the house who loaned them his upper room would gladly have furnished a slave to render this service; but hearing that Jesus was a "Master," he naturally implied that he would bring his own "servant" for this necessary service. Had he entertained any such idea as that a "Master" could find no "servant" willing to render so necessary a service, he must have gladly provided the servant to use the bason and pitcher and water and towel he provided at the door.

Of course, every one of the Twelve saw these implements of menial service as he entered the upper room! But they all detoured around them to their places at the table. Every one of them was determined that he would not be caught with a slave's apron girding his loins and a foot bason in his hands when the kingdom they expected to be launched at any moment should be ushered in. So they sat in their filthy and ill-smelling sandals to eat the Passover with the One they called "Master"—but with their tongues in their cheeks as they said it! They, every one of them, felt themselves too worthy to stoop down and unloose the latchet of His shoes whom they all glibly called "Master." "Ye call me Master and Lord: and ye *say* well; for so I am. If I then, your Lord and Master, have washed your feet; ye also ought to wash one another's feet. For I have given you an example, that ye should do as I have done to you." There was none so low that Christ could not serve that lowly one in the role of slave and drudge and scavenger.

He was a "Godsend" to the world not just as a Guest among men to be entertained by them; not as a tourist to be shown through our homes; not as an exhibit to be marveled at by us; but as a servant—"not to be ministered unto, but to minister, and to give his life a ransom for many." "My meat," he said, "is to do the will of him that sent me, and to finish his work." "I must work the works of him that sent me, while it is day; the night cometh when no man can work. As long as I am in the world, I am the light of the world."

Service a Godsend

I.   Service, therefore, however majestic or menial it may be, is to be regarded by us, who name the Name of Christ, as a Godsend of blessing. Labor was not given to man as a curse in the Garden of Eden. Even before sin entered into the world, man was assigned his labor as a blessing in the form of service, to dress and keep the garden for God. There was a time when work was regarded as a disgrace except for slaves. In our Lord's days in the flesh this heresy of the curse of labor obtained in large degree. Certainly our recent years of depression and mass unemployment have taught us the blessing and privilege of work, even of menial labor entirely outside of the "white collar" category.

But entirely too many professed disciples of Christ have not in them that mind which was in Christ Jesus regarding the glory of serving. "I am among you as he that serveth," said the Master, who also said, "The servant is not above his master." If we call Him "Lord" and "Master" why should we seek exemption from service from which He sought no such exemption? Is it that we wish to be good, but good for nothing? "Verily, verily," He says to us, "The servant is not greater than his Lord: neither he that is sent greater than he that sent him; if ye know these things happy are ye if ye *do* them."

The Only Happy Life

II.   The life of service is, therefore, because it is a "Godsend" of blessing, the only happy life! Who are the happiest people you know? the busy or the idle? Certainly the happiest Christians are the ones who are busiest in the Master's service in His Church. Knowing the truths taught in Bible school, confirmation class and from the pulpit is not enough. We must do something about it. Information must work transformation; impression must work out into expression. We must not only *say* "Master," but we must *be mastered* by Jesus Christ. Our Lord emphasized service in His continual condemnation of the sins of omission above even the sins of commission: "I was hungry, and ye did not give me to eat; I was thirsty, and ye gave me no drink; I was a stranger, and ye took me not in; naked, and ye clothed me not; sick, and in prison, and ye visited me not." To these sinners of omission, good, but good-for-nothing folks, He spoke these words of blistering denunciation, "Depart from me, ye cursed, into the eternal fire which is prepared for the devil and his angels." Those who made themselves a "Godsend" of service "to one of these my brethren, even these least," were the ones He called the "blessed of His Father." To "live and let live" is not nearly enough; to "live and help live," and nothing less than this, is Christian.

The pagan view of success is that of a pyramid with the "big shot" at the top, ministered to and supported by all the rest of men. The Christian view inverts the pyramid and places the great one at the bottom, ministering to all others: "Ye know that the rulers of the Gentiles lord it over them, and their great ones exercise authority over them. Not so shall it be among you: but whosoever would become great among you shall be your minister; and whosoever would be first among you shall be your servant: even as the Son of man came not to be ministered unto, but to minister, and to give his life a ransom for many."

A Symbol of His Incarnation

III.   The girding of Himself with the towel, and the washing of His disciples' feet in the upper room was no isolated flash of pageantry in an effort to dramatize serving love; rather it was the stuff of which all His life and teaching were made up from the manger to the cross, and even on to the throne where "He ever liveth to make intercession for us."

Our Lord's act of humble service in the upper room

as drudge and slave to His disciples is typical of the whole
process of His incarnation. As He arose from supper and
laid aside His garments, so He arose from the bosom of
His Father and laid aside the garment of His deity and
perfect equality with God, to take the form of a servant,
and humbled Himself in that service, not even despising
the shame of the cross. That all of this had in it some
phase of "example, that we should do as He has done," is
taught by Paul in one of the greatest passages in the Scriptures: "Have this mind in you, which was also in Christ
Jesus: who, existing in the form of God, counted not the
being on an equality with God a thing to be grasped, but
emptied himself, taking the form of a servant, being made
in the likeness of men; and being found in fashion as a
man, he humbled himself, becoming obedient even unto
death, yea, the death of the cross."

Are we grasping our dignity, as did the disciples about
the supper table, fearful of losing it in humble service of
our fellow men, or even of our Lord? Christ was rich, but
for our sakes He became poor, that we might be made
rich. He was willing that all His riches should be broken
into the small change of the most menial service to His
inferiors. He spent all He had and all He was for us and
for our redemption.

Not only the way to enjoy being a Christian, but the
very way itself to be a Christian, is to make use of every
opportunity to be of service to Christ, His Church and the

world for which He died, rendering all our service as a thank-offering to Christ, not in any sense to say, "Give me," but always and only to say, "Thank you." There is nothing so thrilling as a life spent in making others happy for Jesus' sake. "Ourselves your servants for Jesus' sake," should be the motto of every one of us as Christians, as it is the motto of our deaconesses.

As our Lord is the best of all "Godsends" to us, He wants us to be "Godsends" to all about us, and to all within the reach of the ministry of our prayers and offerings. As thirty thousand or more of our young people of the United Lutheran Church this week make their solemn confirmation vows and come for the first time to the Lord's Table, let them remember that the blessed fellowship of that sacrament has from the night of its institution carried with it the high privilege and solemn responsibility of service of Christ and His Church. Let them highly resolve to make themselves "Godsends" of serving love in the Church of Christ. Let them find in the Church the field of supreme opportunity to serve the social needs of their community. Let them find there also the supreme opportunity to serve the civic needs of their nation, as they pray and work for a higher type of civic righteousness, and in themselves embody and promulgate that peace on earth and good will toward men which will enthrone Christ in the world as Prince of Peace only as He is so enthroned in the hearts of those who accept and serve Him.

Good Friday

FINISHED

ARMIN GEORGE WENG, PH.D., D.D.
President, The Illinois Synod
CHICAGO, ILLINOIS

The Proper Gospel for

GOOD FRIDAY

When Jesus had spoken these words, he went forth with his disciples over the brook Cedron, where was a garden, into the which he entered, and his disciples. And Judas also, which betrayed him, knew the place: for Jesus ofttimes resorted thither with his disciples. Judas then, having received a band of men and officers from the chief priests and Pharisees, cometh thither with lanterns and torches and weapons. Jesus therefore, knowing all things that should come upon him, went forth. and said unto them, Whom seek ye? They answered him, Jesus of Nazareth. Jesus saith unto them, I am he. And Judas also, which betrayed him, stood with them. As soon then as he had said unto them, I am he, they went backward, and fell to the ground. Then asked he them again, Whom seek ye? And they said, Jesus of Nazareth. Jesus answered, I have told you that I am he: if therefore ye seek me, let these go their way: that the saying might be fulfilled, which he spake, Of them which thou gavest me have I lost none. Then Simon Peter having a sword drew it, and smote the high priest's servant, and cut off his right ear. The servant's name was Malchus. Then said Jesus unto Peter, Put up thy sword into the sheath: the cup which my Father hath given me: shall I not drink it?

Then the band and the captain and officers of the Jews took Jesus, and bound him, and led him away to Annas first; for he was father in law to Caiaphas, which was the high priest that same year. Now Caiaphas was he, which gave counsel to the Jews, that it was expedient that one man should die for the people.

And Simon Peter followed Jesus, and so did another disciple: that disciple was known unto the high priest, and went in with Jesus into the palace of the high priest. But Peter stood at the

174

door without. Then went out that other disciple, which was known unto the high priest, and spake unto her that kept the door, and brought in Peter. Then saith the damsel that kept the door unto Peter, Art not thou also one of this man's disciples? He saith, I am not. And the servants and officers stood there, who had made a fire of coals; for it was cold: and they warmed themselves: and Peter stood with them, and warmed himself.

The high priest then asked Jesus of his disciples, and of his doctrine. Jesus answered him, I spake openly to the world; I ever taught in the synagogue, and in the temple, whither the Jews always resort; and in secret have I said nothing. Why askest thou me? ask them which heard me, what I have said unto them: behold, they know what I said. And when he had thus spoken, one of the officers which stood by struck Jesus with the palm of his hand, saying, Answerest thou the high priest so? Jesus answered him, If I have spoken evil, bear witness of the evil: but if well, why smitest thou me? Now Annas had sent him bound unto Caiaphas the high priest.

And Simon Peter stood and warmed himself. They said therefore unto him, Art not thou also one of his disciples? He denied it, and said, I am not. One of the servants of the high priest, being his kinsman whose ear Peter cut off, saith, Did not I see thee in the garden with him? Peter then denied again: and immediately the cock crew.

Then led they Jesus from Caiaphas unto the hall of judgment: and it was early; and they themselves went not into the judgment hall, lest they should be defiled; but that they might eat the passover. Pilate then went out unto them, and said, What accusation bring ye against this man? They answered and said unto him, If he were not a malefactor, we would not have delivered him up unto thee. Then said Pilate unto them, Take ye him, and judge him according to your law. The Jews therefore said unto him, It is not lawful for us to put any man to death: that the saying of Jesus might be fulfilled, which he spake, signifying what death he should die. Then Pilate entered into the judgment hall again, and called Jesus, and said unto him, Art thou the King of the Jews? Jesus answered him, Sayest thou this thing of thyself, or did others tell it thee of me? Pilate answered, Am I a Jew?

Thine own nation and the chief priests have delivered thee unto me: what hast thou done? Jesus answered, My kingdom is not of this world: if my kingdom were of this world, then would my servants fight, that I should not be delivered to the Jews: but now is my kingdom not from hence. Pilate therefore said unto him, Art thou a king then? Jesus answered, Thou sayest that I am a king? To this end was I born, and for this cause came I into the world, that I should bear witness unto the truth. Every one that is of the truth heareth my voice. Pilate saith unto him, What is truth? And when he had said this, he went out again unto the Jews, and saith unto them, I find in him no fault at all. But ye have a custom, that I should release unto you one at the passover: will ye therefore that I release unto you the King of the Jews? Then cried they all again, saying, Not this man, but Barabbas. Now Barabbas was a robber.

Then Pilate therefore took Jesus, and scourged him. And the soldiers platted a crown of thorns, and put it on his head, and they put on him a purple robe. And said, Hail, King of the Jews! and they smote him with their hands. Pilate therefore went forth again, and saith unto them, Behold, I bring him forth to you, that ye may know that I find no fault in him. Then came Jesus forth, wearing the crown of thorns, and the purple robe. And Pilate saith unto them, Behold the man! When the chief priests therefore and officers saw him, they cried out, saying, Crucify him, crucify him. Pilate saith unto them, Take ye him, and crucify him: for I find no fault in him. The Jews answered him, We have a law, and by our law he ought to die, because he made himself the Son of God.

When Pilate therefore heard that saying, he was the more afraid; and went again into the judgment hall, and saith unto Jesus, Whence are thou? But Jesus gave him no answer. Then saith Pilate unto him, Speakest thou not unto me? knowest thou not that I have power to crucify thee, and have power to release thee? Jesus answered, Thou couldest have no power at all against me, except it were given thee from above: therefore he that delivered me unto thee hath the greater sin. And from thenceforth Pilate sought to release him: but the Jews cried out, saying,

If thou let this man go, thou art not Caesar's friend: whosoever maketh himself a king speaketh against Caesar.

When Pilate therefore heard that saying, he brought Jesus forth, and sat down in the judgment seat in a place that is called the Pavement, but in the Hebrew, Gabbatha. And it was the preparation of the passover, and about the sixth hour: and he saith unto the Jews, Behold your King! And they cried out, Away with him, away with him, crucify him. Pilate saith unto them, Shall I crucify your King? The chief priests answered, We have no king but Caesar. Then delivered he him therefore unto them to be crucified. And they took Jesus and led him away. And he bearing his cross went forth into a place called the place of a skull, which is called in the Hebrew Golgotha: where they crucified him, and two other with him, on either side one, and Jesus in the midst.

And Pilate wrote a title, and put it on the cross. And the writing was, JESUS OF NAZARETH THE KING OF THE JEWS. This title then read many of the Jews: for the place where Jesus was crucified was nigh to the city: and it was written in Hebrew, and Greek, and Latin. Then said the chief priests of the Jews to Pilate, Write not, The King of the Jews; but that he said, I am King of the Jews. Pilate answered, What I have written I have written.

Then the soldiers, when they had crucified Jesus, took his garments, and made four parts, to every soldier a part; and also his coat: now the coat was without seam, woven from the top throughout. They said therefore among themselves, Let us not rend it, but cast lots for it, whose it shall be: that the scripture might be fulfilled, which saith, They parted my raiment among them, and for my vesture they did cast lots. These things therefore the soldiers did.

Now there stood by the cross of Jesus his mother, and his mother's sister, Mary the wife of Cleophas, and Mary Magdalene. When Jesus therefore saw his mother, and the disciple standing by, whom he loved, he saith unto his mother, Woman, behold thy son! Then saith he to the disciple, Behold thy mother! And from that hour that disciple took her unto his own home.

After this, Jesus knowing that all things were now accom-

plished, that the scripture might be fulfilled, saith, I thirst. Now there was set a vessel full of vinegar: and they filled a spunge with vinegar, and put it upon hyssop, and put it to his mouth. When Jesus therefore had received the vinegar, he said, It is finished: and he bowed his head, and gave up the ghost.

The Jews therefore, because it was the preparation, that the bodies should not remain upon the cross on the sabbath day, (for that sabbath day was an high day,) besought Pilate that their legs might be broken, and that they might be taken away. Then came the soldiers, and brake the legs of the first, and of the other which was crucified with him. But when they came to Jesus, and saw that he was dead already, they brake not his legs: but one of the soldiers with a spear pierced his side, and forthwith came there out blood and water. And he that saw it bare record, and his record is true: and he knoweth that he saith true, that ye might believe. For these things were done, that the scripture should be fulfilled, A bone of him shall not be broken. And again another scripture saith, They shall look on him whom they pierced.

*And after this Joseph of Arimathaea, being a disciple of Jesus, but secretly for fear of the Jews, besought Pilate that he might take away the body of Jesus: and Pilate gave him leave. He came therefore, and took the body of Jesus. And there came also Nicodemus, which at the first came to Jesus by night, and brought a mixture of myrrh and aloes, about an hundred pound weight. Then took they the body of Jesus, and wound it in linen clothes with the spices, as the manner of the Jews is to bury. Now in the place where he was crucified there was a garden; and in the garden a new sepulchre, wherein was never man yet laid. There laid they Jesus therefore because of the Jews' preparation day; for the sepulchre was nigh at hand.—*JOHN 18: 1—19: 42.

FINISHED

When Jesus therefore had received the vinegar, he said, It is finished: and he bowed his head, and gave up the ghost.
— JOHN 19: 30.

THE greatest battle ever fought is recorded in Today's Gospel, from which our text is taken. The inspired writer, John, who so well understood our Lord and Saviour, wrote in detail the events of that battle which took the greater part of a night and a day, for he well knew that this battle determined the destiny of mankind. Upon its outcome depended the salvation of the world.

No one can read the story of the treason of Judas, the anguish of Gethsemane, the unfair trial, the desertion of the disciples, the scourging and the crucifixion of Jesus, without emotional stress. How man could be so unjust and so unfair is in striking contrast to the serenity and the patience of Jesus. The contrast between the brutality of man and the comforting and gracious words of Jesus from the cross is too great for anyone to pass over lightly. One shudders as one reads the story of the crucifixion and one is compelled to ask, "How could this be done to the Son of God?" And then one realizes that it is sin—our sin— that did that to Jesus, that caused His suffering and

179

anguish, that nailed Him to the cross. As we look at Him there on the cross, we know that He is dying and suffering in our behalf and in our stead.

To approach calmly and serenely the events of Good Friday is impossible for any Christian. Our emotions are aroused and Jesus captures us as we see Him dying for us. In death as in life, He is victorious. Yes, indeed, the greatest of all battles was fought on Calvary.

The most glorious victory was made known to the world by the cry of Jesus from the cross, "It is finished." This word of Jesus, following the terrible suffering in body, mind and spirit, following the terrible agony suffered by Him who is Son of God and Son of Man, is a word of victory—a victory over sin and death, a victory that found its completion on Easter morn, a victory that completely changed the history of mankind. Just as it is always darkest immediately before the dawn, just so the darkest moment on Good Friday foreshadows the brilliance of the light of Easter morn. When Jesus at the conclusion of His suffering on the cross cried out, "It is finished," it was a call of victory.

As we draw closer to the cross and as this cry rings in our ears, it is only right that we should ask:

What is finished?

So many things are included in this victory call that one cannot enumerate all of them in one sermon. But certain things stand out pre-eminently. For one thing, the life work of Jesus was finished. It was not enough that Jesus taught the way of life in His discourses and in His parables. Had He done only that, then He would truly have been the world's greatest teacher but nothing more. It was not enough that by His life He showed us the way to live. Had He done only that, then He would truly have been the ideal man but nothing more. It was necessary for Him to bear the burden of our sins and our iniquities. He had to drink the bitter cup of suffering to its very dregs. That it was not easy for Him is evidenced by the tense agony in the Garden of Gethsemane. That Jesus was ready and willing to submit to the will of the Father regardless of what that might entail is evidenced by His prayer, "Father, if thou be willing, remove this cup from me: nevertheless, not my will, but thine be done." On the cross Jesus drank this bitter cup. On the cross He suffered the most terrible pain of body and spirit. He did not have to do it but He did it willingly, for He knew it to be the will of His Father. He knew that there was no other way in which the wall between God and man could be broken down; that there was no other way in which God and man could be reconciled. As Luther has so beautifully put it, the world could be saved only by the "holy, precious blood and by the innocent sufferings and death" of the Son of God. But now His life work was done. Triumphantly He could cry, "It is finished."

The prophecy of the Old Testament was finished. All that had been foretold of Him as the One who was to crush the head of the serpent, as the One who was to lead His people out of bondage, as the One who was to take away the sin of the world, all that was fulfilled as Jesus bowed His head in death. The sacrifices of the Old Testament were but shadows of this great sacrifice. Indeed He is the true High Priest. From now on the temple sacrifices were unnecessary. The temple itself was no longer needed—it became but an empty shell—the high priest was no longer needed. The veil of the Temple could now be rent in twain for "It is finished." The salvation of the world was finished. Man was delivered from the bondage of sin. Again he was a child of God. But that could happen only as the Son of God took upon Himself the sin of the world and the burden of man's sin. Evil was vanquished and the world redeemed. The cry, "It is finished," was a cry of trembling joy, the joy of the workman before his finished task, the joy of the artist putting the last touches to his masterpiece, the joy of the conqueror when the trumpets of victory blow. The hopes of humankind through the ages were now fulfilled. The world was redeemed from the bondage of sin. "It is finished."

What blessing this brings to us

With the words of Christ, "It is finished," we have the certainty that we are free from all sin. No longer are we the slaves of sin, no longer are we bound and chained by the power of evil We know that when in an hour of weakness we fall, we can come to God asking His forgiveness for Jesus' sake. The approach to the Father is open. At all times we may come to Him knowing that His hands are outstretched to receive us.

When we think of all that Jesus suffered in our stead and for our sake, we realize the hideousness of sin. It is not something with which to toy, but something from which to flee. To see sin in its full horror we need only to think of Jesus praying in the Garden, with His sweat as though it were great drops of blood. We need only in our mind's eye to see the blood flowing over His holy face from the wounds made by the crown of thorns; we need only to see His back lacerated as a result of the scourging and then to see Him hanging on the cross in our stead, with the nails through His holy hands and feet, suffering inexpressible torture. It is then that we recognize the real nature of sin. As our hearts go out in love to Him who is hanging there, there is within us the firm determination, with the help and guidance of the Holy Spirit, to shun sin and to walk only in the paths of righteousness. As we read it in the explanation of the Second Article of the Creed, "In order that I might be His own, live under Him in His Kingdom, and serve Him in everlasting righteousness, innocence and blessedness."

The cry of Jesus also comforts us in our suffering. We

must enter into the Kingdom of Heaven after many tribulations. Often our cross seems almost too heavy to bear, but when we look at Calvary we know that with God's help we can carry our burdens, for we know that the time will come when there will be no burden to bear, when also we can say, "It is finished." We look toward the Father's House where the many mansions are. When the cold hand of death shall come upon us we will look with full confidence to the cross of Christ. Then with the Apostle we can say, "I have fought a good fight," and with the Martyr Stephen we will say, "Lord Jesus, receive my spirit."

The greatest battle ever fought was the battle on Golgotha. It was a battle fought for us by our Saviour. Had the battle been lost, then there would have been no hope for us at all. But thanks be to God, Jesus won the victory, and His call of triumph is also our cry of victory. The greatest victory the world has ever seen is that announced by the words of Jesus, "It is finished."

Good Friday

THE SEVEN WORDS FROM THE CROSS

HENRY CORNEHLSEN, JR., S.T.M.
St. John's Church
EASTON, PENNSYLVANIA

THE SEVEN WORDS FROM THE CROSS

BEHIND the simple grandeur of the seven last utterances of Jesus is the glowing heart of Jesus. It is beating with a tenderness and an affection that make even the suffering to be almost forgotten. It has told its secret countless times before, but it can never tell it all nor does it ever tell it the same. "Oh, Jerusalem, I would have gathered you . . ." "Oh, Peter . . . I have prayed for you." "Wilt thou also go away?" "Zaccheus, come down." "Lazarus, come forth." It is the secret of a heart that cared.

But not only in fashion of humanist: else with full heart growing sadder, it might easily be that

> "You sit apart; entrenched in primeval gloom
> Before futility's vacant shrine you bow.
> You can never feel the stir in the ancient womb
> Of Time nor touch the pulse of the vibrant Now."

Jesus' glowing heart dealt not with despair as men left Him, for therein was His vivid sense of the reality of God. Think of knowing God as Jesus knew Him! Think of meeting death, as we all must, with the knowledge of God that Jesus had! Let us journey once more to Golgotha and learn what it means to care for man, to trust in God.

THE FIRST WORD

Father, forgive them; for they know not what they do.
—LUKE 23: 34.

THE heavens, as I write this, are being tinted with the morning light. Before me are the dunes of a South Carolina beach. The sea stretches out holding infinity of number and of motion in its waves. Lo, the sea reaches an end, yet not an end as it dips below the horizon from which a golden sun appears. It is dawn! A new day has begun in God's world. Nothing petty can live in the pageantry of the Creator's dawn. Only noble thoughts, glorious deeds, sweeping obedience, splendor of God can exist! Thus it is with this word of forgiveness born in that heart of yearning and of faith. A new day had come for man's humanity to man.

Cries of hate have been filling the air. Nation has been distrusting nation. The greatest slaughter is being considered the greatest victory. Dunkirk, Pearl Harbor, Hong Kong! Remember! Remember! It was on Calvary, too, the Roman oppressor of His people stood before Jesus. The spittle was hardly dry on His cheek where a soldier had crudely forgotten the divine image that he

possessed, too. Or was it that no one had ever told him?
Plaudits and taunts were all intermingled. Yet to Him
who would never break a bent reed or extinguish the
smoking flax, the children's high Hosannas seemed more
insistent on the memory than the guttural "Crucify."—
"Father, forgive them."

And you? Remember we can never be sinned against
as Jesus was. Even if we are awakened—rudely and
crudely—to the fact that we are a negro—by God's will
—in New York, Philadelphia, or New Orleans; or some
Nisei—by God's will—in San Pedro, whose home, according to one old Christian Nisei, may be "in storage" for the
duration, but his faith is not, for with old eyes still alight,
he smilingly says, "What we do? I do not know but we
are not afraid, for we are Christians."

Jesus forgave, and He bids us forgive. We cannot be
right with God and wrong with our brother. Has anyone
wronged us? It is our *privilege* to forgive. Have we
wronged another? It is our *privilege* to seek reconciliation.
After all, most of us have so *little* to forgive. Most of us
have never been deeply wronged. What was it caused the
quarrel, the coldness, the separation, and severed the
friendship? A little taunt, an unkind word, a hasty remark,
a false-or-true accusation, a supposed social slight, a mis-
understanding. How paltry and trivial and insignificant
all of them put together seem when we stand before the
Cross of Christ. When we think of all the malice, the jeal-

ousy, envy, spite, blasphemy, and heartless cruelty revealed there—all poured out, without cause, upon the innocent Head of the spotless Son of God, who had proved Himself the best friend of mankind! Yet He forgave.

Jesus came to save, to bring peace to human souls. He knew they did not totally understand. How could they? His mission was His very life. His blood outpoured was the price He paid for His yearning and His trust. The world could not give or take away the peace He brought. But man and nation, forgiven of Him, could forgive and open the way to His peace.

> "Peace, perfect peace, in this dark world of sin?
> The blood of Jesus whispers peace within."

THE SECOND WORD

Verily I say unto thee, Today shalt thou be with me in paradise.—LUKE 23: 43.

ONLY one who cares deeply for others, with utter forgetfulness of self, with a kind of divine abandonment, could have uttered this second word. One could easily see only a criminal, a man outside the pale of respectability, of not much if any use to the world if he were saved. Or going further, one might say that he would be an odd sort of character to be taken to Paradise. Yet how strange the assortment there really is—Abraham, Enoch, David, Rahab, Mary Magdalene, Mary the Mother,

Zacchaeus, the Woman of Samaria, the Thief on the cross, Stephen! One thing I do know. The angels in heaven rejoiced. A thief on the cross but a man for all that, who forgot his own agony to bear witness for a good man before his fellow criminal, became a friend of Jesus on that cross. What possibilities for nobility were in this thief! He knew the virtue of fairness. "We receive our punishment justly, the due reward of our deeds: but this man has done nothing amiss."

Dead wood! The phrase is a reprehensible one to a Christian who has hope and faith and love. No one with the breath of life can be in that category, not even a criminal in his last agonies on his cross. In the "Tale of Two Cities," the coward, the ne'er-do-well, but one who still has the wick that smokes, the reed that is unbroken, a soul with the unextinguishable divine spark, substitutes himself to save another's life. As he goes to the guillotine, he says, "I am doing something finer than I have ever done before, I go to a greater rest than I have ever known!" The true Christian never sees his fellow man only as he is but as he might be. Hope is one of the abiding characteristics, and does spring eternal in the human breast.

Churchmanship is not just getting to heaven. It is leading the fallen and falling out of hell. Even in our last hours, if by no other way than indirect influence—the great and glorious possibility of mellow and consecrated old age—one can be leading the damned out of hell.

Churchmanship is not just being saved from our sins. It is saving people from those vices which are in the world of the outer darkness, from which come the maimed and the dumb and the blind and the deaf. This second word would have us nerved from day to day, with our own yearning, trusting heart, with intercessory intentions and acts and influences, that man shall do right because we did.

Jesus was dying as the Saviour of the world, but He did not forget one solitary individual. There never would be a "cry in the night with nothing but a cry." There is a corner of God's heart for each of us. Never must we be too busy, never must we have too much self-pity; never must we be too interested in the organization to forget its reason for being; never so concerned over budgets and crowds to neglect that one cry of that one sheep lost on the way. "Go and show John again those things ye do hear and see."

"Peace, perfect peace, by thronging duties pressed?
To do the will of Jesus, this is rest."

THE THIRD WORD

Woman, behold thy son!—Behold thy mother!
—JOHN 19: 26, 27.

HERE was no Saviour of the World who neglected a neighbor, no Queen of Russia weeping as a play progressed and her coachman froze outside. Here was not a man lost in the maze of a forest unable to see the trees.

Jesus, we have noticed, amid His plans for the soul of the world remembered the soul of a man. Likewise, amid His plans for spiritual salvation, He did not forget man had a human body and affections and yearnings—that man had to live, to eat, to have companionship. There was no losing of Himself or expecting others merely to lose themselves on a pillar like Simeon Stylites, and then as a parasite upon society, expect the world to take care of the mystic elect.

A grave sin of mankind is the sin of impersonality. It is the sin of the careless, the praying egoist who lacks this yearning, trusting heart of Jesus. He was interested in the individual welfare of man. Sorrows may abound in the deluge, yet Jesus is there, a haven of rest for you of "more value than many sparrows," you "the very hairs of whose head are numbered." This is Jesus' way—to see the unrealized potentialities, the unexpressed needs of other souls, rich and poor, educated and ignorant, black and yellow and white, attractive stranger or familiar relative—one of the most difficult things in the world. Christianity thus becomes one of the hardest of all religions to put into practice: the hardest—and at the same time the noblest challenge.

Jesus became His mother's Saviour. In the home frequently lies the hardest test of our Christianity. Amid our relatives is frequently our great ordeal as a Christian spirit, to keep on radiating love in spite of an aunt or an uncle, of going on in spite of a father or a mother, of rising to new spiritual heights in spite of a husband or a wife, to find in the *home* a beauty that is real, to find in the circumstances of one's life from day to day a challenge that is heroic, to be able to turn the magic of one's soul upon what may be common and sordid, and to illumine it with the heavenly light. Salvation can come into our very home because we have made our Christianity vital and real, by our patience, by our courtesy, by our tenderness, by our self-sacrifice, by our faith, by our smiling submission to all the petty tyrannies of an unconsecrated family relationship.

This sin of impersonality which begins frequently in the home can extend to nations. In one of his shrewd essays in "The Olive Tree," Aldous Huxley points out the treachery of our common habit of talking about wars and battles in terms of so many "rifles" and "machine guns," in terms of "lines of force" and "turning the flank" and "man power." We make wars abstract and remove the personality from thousands of fathers and sons who are plain, decent human beings put into uniform, and so we conveniently ignore the folly and barbarity of war. The sin of impersonality is the root cause of all man's inhumanity to man. At the cross, nothing is impersonal. Human souls are remembered. A robber is saved, a mother is cared for, a disciple is remembered.

You who know the peace of Jesus; you who hear with

chaos round about, the word "Peace, be still" within the soul as the sea of life fills with storms, you are to be the yearning, caring, trusting one making for your home, your loved ones and for a desperate world an incarnate Christianity by your thoughtfulness and self-sacrifice.

> "Peace, perfect peace, with sorrows surging round?
> On Jesus' bosom nought but calm is found."

THE FOURTH WORD

My God, my God, why hast thou forsaken me?
—MATTHEW 27: 46.

WHY do waves never cease at the shore? Whence come the tides? In us there is a hunger for values. We crave knowledge, we crave beauty in color, form, sound, movement. We crave moral excellence without which a man finds no peace for his soul. But who can put his finger on the mundane cause of this hunger for value? No anthropologist can say that in such and such an era the need for values was born in man.

There is another mystery, of spiritual as well as of mental dimensions—the fourth utterance from the cross. Who can fathom its depths? The words express the real pressure on Jesus' soul of the enormous burden of the world's sin, suffering, and for the time being, silence of God. It is an awe-inspiring, dreadful word; yet one of the most precious of all in its extraordinary nature. No friend would invent it. Impressed by Jesus' divinity, not desiring to allow any doubt to enter, a friend might easily reluctantly reveal it. It is the only one of the seven recorded utterances from the cross given us in the first two Gospels. Thus for some years the early Church had in writing no other word but this cry of anguish, of a distress of mind endured by our Lord. Here is another proof of the authenticity of the Gospel Record.

Unholy exultation may easily have greeted this word. Jesus was always so sure. Now it is all over. Let us be off. The crowd began to leave to discuss the various incidents and to wonder who of the Jewish agitators might be next.

It is precious, too, because we realize again that God was in Christ reconciling the world unto Himself. We do not understand fully but we know it means our redemption. I do not understand electricity, but this service is being conducted by means of electricity. Even though my sins be as scarlet, lo, the Lord will "purge me with hyssop, and I shall be clean: wash me and I will be whiter than snow." But that redemption costs. Jesus was "the Lamb of God that taketh away the sin of the world." No, we will not increase the agony of that separation by thoughtless, careless sin upon our part.

> "O the deep, deep love of Jesus,
>   Vast, unmeasured, boundless, free;
> Rolling as a mighty ocean
>   In its fulness over me;

> Underneath me, all around me,
>   Is the current of His love;
> Flowing through me, leading homeward,
>   To the glorious rest above."

It is so precious to us because this word was a question that Jesus asked of God. Jesus knew what it was to ask "Why?" Even He, spotless Lamb of God, questioned and sought a reason. Thus when through sufferings or thwartings of life's cherished ambitions, in some period of desolation, we cry out, "Why, Lord, why?" lo, the comfort of the Shepherd in sympathetic understanding is ours: "I know, beloved, I know. Have faith." *Apres la neige et la pluie, le beau temps!* "After the snow and the rain the beautiful weather."

> "Peace, perfect peace, with loved ones far away?
> In Jesus' keeping we are safe and they."

THE FIFTH WORD

I thirst.—JOHN 19: 28.

JESUS was offered a potion twice. One He refused. The other time He accepted. That which was refused was the medicated potion-wine mingled with myrrh—the intention of which was to deaden pain; and therefore when it was presented to the Saviour, it was rejected. The reason commonly assigned for that seems to be the true one. The Son of Man would not meet death in a state of stupefaction. He chose to meet His God awake.

It was not merely to be awake and suffer as much pain as possible, the greater the hero to be. Such a thought is almost blasphemous. He desired to conquer not through the flesh but through the spirit. He might by anodyne escape from suffering, but He came to conquer it, not to escape. But note the vinegar or sour wine was accepted as a refreshing draught, for it would seem that He did not look upon the value of the suffering as consisting in this, that He should make it as exquisite as possible, but rather that He should not suffer one drop of the cup of agony which His Father had put into His hand to trickle down the side untasted. But neither would He make to Himself one drop more of suffering than His Father had given.

To suffer pain for others without flinching—that is our Master's example; but pain for the mere sake of pain —that is not Christian; to accept poverty in order to do good for others—that is our Saviour's principle; but to become poor for the sake and merit of being poor is but selfishness after all.

The cult of comfort! What a temptation it is! Are not too many dreaming of the new order as the old order with no priorities, low taxes, fine cars, plenty of sugar, tires, and travel? The new order must have in it an element of unselfishness, of service to man, of sacrifice for man. It is for us in the spirit of the yearning, thirsting Jesus, to endure suffering for Him. Men and women are walking through the world as through the valley of the shadow of death. One need only to read or to see that books and conversations throw no light upon the message of the Master. Man is forgetting he is a son of the living God, that God yearns and woos and hunts for him and His Voice is round him like a "bursting sea." Appalling masses of people have banished God from their universe "for the duration."

Jesus thirsted for the world. He loved the world. We know that. He loved Judas. He would have taken him back in an instant if Judas had come to the Cross and said: "I am brokenhearted at what I have done." He would have taken Pontius Pilate, Caiaphas. He would have taken them all. Now, however, He was dying and nothing to show for His life in many results. What had He to show? He had come down attended by angels singing Gloria in excelsis. Now a few sorrowing women and one disciple. What else has He obtained? As He looks over the world, over nations and cities and factories, or amid the snows of Russia, Ceylon's Isle, India's coral strand, under the stars on a clear night over the English Channel, or at the bottom of the sea? In Russia it will not be the skiers at their sport but men killing and dying; in Ceylon not the songs of women sorting tea but the wails of the bereaved; in India not the dance of joy but the silence of anxiety; not bluebirds over Dover but bombers. His cry, "I thirst," is a crushing disappointment. Did you ever set your heart on one thing and not get it? Like Him, you in your disappointments, must learn to be humble and simple, and brave and frank. You must admit a disappointment. But then even if life seems empty, what you prayed for, worked for, wanted, sweated for gone—then to say and feel, "I'll carry on. I'll wait,"—thus would Jesus.

It is for us, unafraid and undaunted, to become the healer and the comforter, to endure the scorn and the taunts and the persecution if need be. The bishops of Norway with the light that Stephen knew in their eyes will tell you. We must let no tears of self-pity, even from honest and deep suffering and sorrow wash away the lilies of Easter time. Our lamentations must not drown the song of the birds of the garden where Jesus and Mary walked with a new understanding.

> "Peace, perfect peace, our future all unknown?
> Jesus we know and He is on the throne."

THE SIXTH WORD

It is finished.—JOHN 19: 30.

HE was just a lad with an idea in that early teen age of idealism. It proved to be a divine compulsion but did He know it was such? Was He conscious of angel voices like a Joan of Arc, or of an inner voice like a Samuel? A seed was there of a life never to be equaled by mortal man. A mother's question brought forth its oral prophecy that led from a carpenter's bench to a cross, from an event in time to a condition of eternity, "Wist ye not that I must be about my Father's business?"

So many little things must have filled up that life to bring it to its tragic and glorious end. Must he stay on in His father's house when the world seemed to beckon Him? Surely not beyond the age of twenty? Oh, He wanted to aid mankind. "Father, let me go." "Not yet, not yet." Then those eternities of days in the wilderness! He had waited so long. Was there to be no short cut now for aiding man? "Yes," Satan said, "there might be." Jesus knew then there would not, could not be. "Get thee behind me, Satan." But must it be such bitter dregs? "Oh, Father, may this cup—but not my will but Thine be done." Thus, always, ever and ever!

"It is finished!" What is finished? The life of perfect obedience, built up from day to day decisions, choices that had to be made. It was the old thought, deed, act, habit, character, destiny progression; a youth's ideal into a life's purpose into a destiny for the soul of the world. Little things! Remember it is not the spectacular display at holiday seasons that reveals one's character, but the day-by-day courtesies, hour-by-hour kindnesses, and week-by-week fidelities which lay bare one's inmost soul. To stand uncomplainingly before some tiny barrier; to walk patiently amid reversals; to toil without reward; to labor without return; to endure without bitterness—in times such as these the soul of man is revealed. The purpose of the meadow is to provide clover, but it is the smell of new-mown hay which makes you love it. The purpose of life is to fulfill its mission, but it is the day-by-day kindnesses and the common courtesies in small annoyances and trivial incidents which make character winsome. Florence Nightingale, going about her commonplace tasks with lantern in hand in the barracks of Scutaria, never dreamed that men would kiss the shadow her lantern cast upon the wall. "When saw we thee an hungered and fed thee, Lord?"

> "God pity all the lonely folk
> With grief they do not tell
> Women waking in the night
> And men dissembling well.
> God pity all the brave who go
> The common road, and wear
> No ribboned medals on their breasts
> No laurels in their hair."

In His last moments, when the mist is gathering, and the cold stream of death is calling upon Him to cross it, and the end awaits Him, He has still the strength to cry, "It is finished." He was obedient to His Father's voice. His life became a salvation for man. This life proved more precious than rubies and diamonds to despairing souls, for it tells us that the life that loves God and man, with a yearning, trusting heart, is a complete life, wherever it commences and wherever it closes, be it manger to cross or otherwise. It tells us that the divinest life may be lived in the shortest hours. If we could live our little lives, stirred by this conviction, what genuine happiness, what abiding peace, what holy enthusiasm, would be ours!

When you say as your life ends, "It is finished," may it be likewise, with courage, a life that amidst the disappointments, despondencies, the defeats of life, was true to truth, conforming to conscience, daring to do your duty, possibly frequently failing, but never being a failure. God's heroes are those not afraid to fail, to die on a cross for a good cause. The Father's business!

> "Peace, perfect peace, death shadowing us and ours?
> Jesus has vanquished death and all its powers."

THE SEVENTH WORD

Father, into thy hands I commend my spirit.—LUKE 23: 46.

HERE is already a cry of victory. This is no longer death but life. The darkness of the fourth utterance was but momentary. For that moment the Redeemer had felt alone and deserted, and then in the midst of it, He cried out, "Father, into thy hands I commend my spirit." In this instance He realized His inseparable union with the Father. I think of the words of that great American writer, Thomas Wolfe, who said:

"To lose the earth you know, for greater knowing; to lose the life you have for greater life; to find a land . . . more large than earth—toward which the conscience of the world is tending—a wind is rising, and the rivers flow."

The crucifix with its cruelty is already turning into a cross of hope. The veil is rent. The holy of holies of the eternal kingdom is ours to know. In the Father's hands! What peace is there! No agony of death! As we descend the hill of meditation into the world of action, we must take the spirit of Jesus with us. Certain shafts of light come from His radiant spirit so manifest to us again through these seven words.

Jesus, we note, kept His faith simple. It was so different from the rules and regulations of His time. No wonder the people said when they heard Him speak, "Whence hath this man His wisdom? We have never heard anyone speak like Him." The common people heard Him gladly. People were the better for the sound of His voice and the sight of Him talking, mainly because He was a simple, free man. This last word is like the word of a little child falling asleep in His Father's arms. Simple and grand were His birth, His life, His death.

This sense of God was a lifetime matter with Jesus. We call it prayer. Prayer is more than a formula of devotion. It is a daily program. No day can have God in it that does not begin with the sense of the relationship between ourselves and God as sons and a Father. However wrong yesterday was, however much we may have marred it, we must not allow the sense of yesterday's failure to interfere with the joy of the awakening hour that is in the opening sentence of the Lord's Prayer. As a child, it is our baptism: "In the Name of the Father"; as a confirmand, it is our blessing: "The Father in heaven for Jesus' sake"; as a Christian it is our daily salutation to a Friend Who never faileth; as a believer entering heaven's portals, it is our open sesame, our password to glory: "Father!" So simple is a Christian's faith.

This word shows in retrospect Jesus' obedience to the Father. He could only use the word because man was ever His brother. Prayer has little value for itself alone. The Lord's prayers were plural prayers. "Father, I pray for them. . . . I pray not that thou shouldest take them out of the world, but that thou shouldest keep them from the evil."

> "These are my people—octoroon
> Or white or yellow as harvest moon,
> Your people, our people, everyone,
> Brothers beneath the beneficent sun,
> Brothers through ice or tropic rain,
> Brothers in laughter, brothers in pain."

Whatever we want for ourselves, we must also want for others. We will have nothing, as Whitman cried, on any terms whatsoever save those of common brotherhood with the rest of mankind. We do not ask for special privileges, special graces, special exemptions. Before the cross, we cannot. We will not be afraid. We will not creep past. No, even as conquerors of a war, for peace that lasts, this shall be our stand.

Lo, I see and comprehend more clearly the joy of Jesus, that for the joy set before Him He endured the cross, suffering the shame. Oh, witnesses at the cross, followers of Jesus, all day long we can carry the thought, "Children of God!" With this thought, the gates of hell shall not prevail against us. Our enemies who misunderstood us cannot harm us. All they who seek to do us evil shall be vanquished, because the mantle of our Father's love is over us and His banner is above our heads.

Let us in the Divine Presence of the Fatherhood of God and the brotherhood of man, oh

> "Let us plant our feet on the highway
>   Along with broken men,
> Who are marching across the ages
>   Over and over again.
> For never until we have fathomed
>   The anguish of flesh and soul
> Can we gather the titan power
>   To make humanity whole."

> "It is enough: earth's struggles soon shall cease,
> And Jesus call us to heaven's perfect peace."

Saturday in Holy Week
"...AND BURIED"

HERBERT A. BOSCH
Concordia Church
BUFFALO, NEW YORK

The Proper Gospel for

SATURDAY IN HOLY WEEK

When the even was come, there came a rich man of Arima-thaea, named Joseph, who also himself was Jesus' disciple: he went to Pilate, and begged the body of Jesus. Then Pilate commanded the body to be delivered. And when Joseph had taken the body, he wrapped it in a clean linen cloth, and laid it in his own new tomb, which he had hewn out in the rock: and he rolled a great stone to the door of the sepulchre, and departed. And there was Mary Magdalene, and the other Mary, sitting over against the sepulchre.

*Now the next day, that followed the day of the preparation, the chief priests and Pharisees came together unto Pilate, saying, Sir, we remember that that deceiver said, while he was yet alive, After three days I will rise again. Command therefore that the sepulchre be made sure until the third day, lest his disciples come by night, and steal him away, and say unto the people, He is risen from the dead: so the last error shall be worse than the first. Pilate said unto them, Ye have a watch: go your way, make it as sure as ye can. So they went, and made the sepulchre sure, sealing the stone, and setting a watch.—*MATTHEW 27: 57-66.

"...AND BURIED"

And when Joseph had taken the body, he wrapped it in a clean linen cloth, and laid it in his own new tomb, which he had hewn out in the rock: and he rolled a great stone to the door of the sepulchre, and departed.

So they went and made the sepulchre sure, sealing the stone, and setting the watch.—MATTHEW 27: 59, 60, 66.

THERE is always something majestic about the Creed, as it is confessed from week to week. On occasions without number and by a countless host, the phrases are uttered with a certain magnificent eloquence, until the words are spoken, "He was crucified, dead and buried." Then the tempo slackens, voices are hushed to a degree, and there is a brief pause of an almost dramatic quality. It seems that the Church not only gives oral assent to, but at that very moment indicates mental appreciation of the humiliation of Him, "Who became obedient unto death, even the death of the cross . . ." In a most solemn cadence we say, "He was crucified, . . . dead, . . . and buried."

It is about the Burial of Our Lord, that we speak today, with special reference to the 59th, 60th and 66th verses of Matthew 27.

I—*The Secret Disciple*

When the cruel ordeal of crucifixion was at last ended, the bodies of executed malefactors were customarily left exposed, as a kind of last indignity heaped upon the condemned. The gruesome business over, no other duties claimed the attention of the soldiery: burial of the criminal was surely not their concern. Yet friends might brave the mockery of public opinion and meet the contempt of ruthless officials to claim the broken bodies of legal victims. They then could give them such decent burial, as circumstances might permit. A friend like this was Joseph of Arimathaea. Because he was a disciple in secret, he came forward at this hour, desired the Body, and receiving Pilate's permission, arranged for its burial. The necessity for the immediate removal of the Body before the Great Day, and the longing to provide honorable burial for his Friend prompted the belated acknowledgment of loyalty and called forth the tardy expression of friendship.

All of the Evangelists add strokes and colors to the portrait of this man presented in the Gospels. Joseph is a man of wealth and position: he is the "rich counsellor." He is a man of character and principle: "honorable . . . good man and just"; with convictions that will not yield: "He had not consented to the counsel and deed of them." He is a man of religious yearnings and capacities: "he waited for the Kingdom of God" . . . and was Jesus' disciple. It was this man who desired the Body of Jesus. . . .

And is it not significant that Joseph is remembered by posterity and honored by the Church, not for his position nor his possessions, but for his discipleship and for the last tender ministry to our Lord?

II—*The Sepulchre*

With the aid of Nicodemus and other unnamed friends, the Body is taken from the Cross. In Rubens' "Descent from the Cross" we have a vivid picture of this labor of love as eight or nine persons toil, bearing the body, heavy in death. The spices have been prepared, the ointment is ready as the limbs and the frame are swathed in the linen cloths; and the mournful procession wends its way graveward. To the sepulchre the sacred burden is borne. The vault is spacious; intended no doubt originally to receive the bodies of Joseph and his family, it is as yet unused. This garden becomes the first Christian cemetery and the tomb, hewn out of rock, is the first Christian grave. The Son of Man, "who had not where to lay his head," poor and despised as He was, is "with the rich in his death"— and thus an ancient prophecy is fulfilled. The last detail of the bitter duty is completed, as the huge stone, of a size sufficient to block the entrance, is rolled into place,—that the quiet precincts shall not be violated, nor the lifeless body stolen. Then with anguish of heart, they depart, spirits crushed to the ground.

III—*The Seal*

As Joseph and his assistants are thus occupied, and as some of the women look on, the enemies of our Lord also witness the strange proceedings. Surprised no doubt, that one of Joseph's standing shall thus pay tribute to the object of their hatred, they are puzzled; they wonder whether other precautions are not necessary. The Man of Nazareth is dead, of course. The Disciples are scattered, true. But will they gather courage, and in the darkness come to steal that Body? Will they then announce His Resurrection? Will they not defy us, as they triumphantly recall His statement and point to the grave, from which He has vanished? Perhaps we had better make assurance doubly sure.

So to Pilate they hurry. That impostor, they say, made some rash assertions. If put to death, He was going to rise again. We know that that cannot happen. But we are not sure of His men. They might plot fraud. They could steal His body. And they could point to the empty grave, as though He had come to life. That would make a bad situation worse. It might lead to trouble. For us, and for you, too! The people would be upset. So, for the sake of law and order, we come with another request. Put your seal upon the grave. Order the guard out to watch the tomb. Just for three days. That will be our common protection, and all trouble will be avoided. . . . You will? . . . Thank you, Sir.

So across the entrance to the tomb, and connecting sepulchre with the stone, threads and thongs are drawn, upon which the seal of the governor is impressed. Weak threads, yes! But the seal? Strong and sure, signifying that the tomb is under the authority of the empire, whose power none ventures to question, and whose seal none dares to break. . . . "So they went, and made the sepulchre sure, sealing the stone and setting the watch." Thus the melancholy task is performed. Jesus is crucified, . . . and dead, . . . and buried;—and the note of mourning is dominant in the heart of the Church today.

*   *   *   *

But there are two considerations which shed light through the darkness, and dissipate the intensity of the gloom. The first is the announcement of the Resurrection. We know that "Christ will not be holden of death," and that He emerges victoriously to Life. His cause has not collapsed, nor is His purpose thwarted. The unique character of His Person and Work and the tremendous significance of His Resurrection can be realized in part in the following contrast:

On the thirtieth of March, 1928, the people of Delaware, Ohio, gathered in public meeting both to honor a distinguished fellow citizen, and to announce his candidacy for the presidential nomination of the Republican party. There were banners and bunting; flowers and flags; placards and pictures; slogans and streamers; the blare of bands cushioned the excited tones of hundreds of voices. Applause and confidence, eagerness and enthusiasm reigned, but the nomination "Willis for President" was never made. For the Senator, even as he was in the corridor of the Gray Chapel of Ohio Wesleyan University, and was about to enter the stage door to deliver his address, was fatally stricken; and in a few brief moments, before he could be rushed to a hospital, the aspiring candidate was an expiring soul. His cause collapsed,—and down came banners and bunting, placards and pictures; muted was the noise of the band. Scattered were his cohorts,—crushed and dispersed were his friends. A corpse for President? Never! Similarly we ask: A lifeless Jesus, the author and finisher of our faith? Impossible. But because of what occurred on the Third Day, because of the many infallible proofs, the burial did not write "Finis" to the Life of Christ, and we know that Jesus did rise from the dead. From that time until now as "Saviour of Men," "Christ, the Friend of Sinners," "Son of God, Redeemer of the World" and as "Jesus, the Way, the Truth and the Life" He is proclaimed, living and regnant at the right hand of God and in the hearts of men forever.

The second consideration is the boundless scope and potential beauty of any deed of loving service, done for Christ. Joseph "wrought in sad sincerity" yet his name is honored as are only few names in the early Church. The burial has forever linked his name with that of the Crucified, has given rise to legend and has called forth a literature and drama, which has edified and inspired. The versions of the "Holy Grail" in Europe and the "Vision of Sir Launfal" in America have retold the ageless story. They still declare that an honest service in devoted love for the Saviour is never lost: it can gather richness through the years. Through Joseph we are reminded again:

"How far that little candle throws his beams!
So shines a good deed in a cruel world."

Easter Day

MY REDEEMER LIVETH!

BEHREND MEHRTENS
Trinity Church
New Haven, Connecticut

The Proper Gospel for

EASTER

And when the sabbath was past, Mary Magdalene, and Mary the mother of James, and Salome, had bought sweet spices, that they might come and anoint him. And very early in the morning the first day of the week, they came unto the sepulchre at the rising of the sun. And they said among themselves, Who shall roll us away the stone from the door of the sepulchre? And when they looked, they saw that the stone was rolled away: for it was very great. And entering into the sepulchre, they saw a young man sitting on the right side, clothed in a long white garment; and they were affrighted. And he saith unto them, Be not affrighted: Ye seek Jesus of Nazareth, which was crucified: he is risen; he is not here: behold the place where they laid him. But go your way, tell his disciples and Peter that he goeth before you into Galilee: there shall ye see him, as he said unto you. And they went out quickly, and fled from the sepulchre; for they trembled and were amazed: neither said they any thing to any man; for they were afraid.—MARK 16: 1-8.

MY REDEEMER LIVETH!

THE gospel for Easter Day brings us the good news that Christ is risen, and gives us the assurance that we are redeemed from sin, from death, and from the power of the devil; "in order that we might be His, live under Him in His Kingdom, and serve Him in everlasting righteousness, innocence and blessedness; even as He is risen from the dead and lives and reigns to all eternity."

There are those who regard this gospel as incredible. There are others who believe it is irrelevant today. But incredible as it may sound, it has yet to be proven false; and irrelevant as it may seem, it has implications of tremendous importance for our day. In the absence of evidence to deny the truth of it, we need not spend time establishing reasons for our faith in it. We can confidently affirm that the Lord is risen indeed, and devote our time to implications of the gospel, if haply they might reflect glory to God and contribute to the enrichment and enhancement of life.

Think of the people who are in the situation the

women of the gospel were in, when they came to the sepulchre at the rising of the sun, the first Easter Day, wondering who would roll them away the stone from the door of the sepulchre. They are the people who stand helpless in the presence of their problem. They do not know how to overcome the obstacle in the way to the achievement of their purpose. The magnitude of their difficulty overwhelms them. They wonder who there may be to help them out of their situation. They are thwarted, and it makes them anxious and apprehensive. They have been disappointed and disillusioned, and it would not take much to make them despair. They are in the mood of the women, who said among themselves, "Who shall roll us away the stone from the door of the sepulchre?"

Not that these people are not abroad doing some deed of loving service and devotion, even as the women were. But that they are the victims of futile fear. For it is recorded of the women that "when they looked, they saw that the stone was rolled away." How it was done is not related. Nor does it matter, so long as the inference is clear. Obviously, it means that the women had no need to worry, and, therefore, the people in their situation today are torturing themselves with needless anxiety. They are forever wondering who will roll them away the stone; whereas, if they would only look, they would see that it was rolled away, even though "it was very great."

In other words, if people only would trust God and

not worry, do what they can in accordance with His will, where action is possible, and confidently leave in His hands situations they cannot control, they would be free from fear and grim forebodings and in a position to enjoy life more abundantly.

Happy is the man, who in his anxious and apprehensive moments, can say with Job of old, "I know that my Redeemer liveth." He has the assurance of a power to overcome fear, and possesses a sure hope of salvation. And yet, sad to say, even that man at times yields to fear and worry.

It is one thing, when people are anxious and apprehensive, but, like the women in the gospel, unaware at the moment that their Redeemer liveth; then there is at least some semblance of reason for their anxiety and apprehensiveness. But it is quite another thing, when a person says, "I know that my Redeemer liveth," and yields to anxiety and apprehension notwithstanding.

There may be, and undoubtedly are, people who can neither acquire the power to overcome fear nor cherish the hope of salvation. For conceivably a man may be the victim of a situation, which by its very nature may inhibit his ability to lay hold of the divine means of release at his disposal, and there may be no power under heaven to help him out of his situation. My heart goes out to such a man, and my prayers ascend in his behalf, if haply God might send him speedy deliverance from his affliction. He is quite different from the man who feigns a helpless situation to gratify his ego or to escape his responsibilities in life. I have no use for him. He is a despicable fellow, and is not entitled to any help human or divine.

I know, too, that there are people who have not fully mastered the art of trusting God implicitly, and others who have not the slightest notion of what it means to trust Him. The man who comes through gloriously in a crisis, but completely "goes to pieces" under the petty strains of life, is an example of the first group, while the man who stoically resigns himself to his situation, and blindly, if not blandly, accepts it as his fate, is a representative of the second.

But I am not troubled by the plight of any of these people so much as I am baffled by the inconsistency of those of us who profess faith in the Saviour, and do not live out our faith in the situations which daily confront us. Ever so many of us have right within our reach means which God has placed there for our help; but, if we do not misuse or abuse them, we either fail to recognize them as given of God, and keep waiting for some miraculous or cataclysmic intervention of God, or we utterly disregard them, and then accuse God of denying us His help.

We make a mistake, when we assume that God will help us by suddenly removing our problem or by giving us some miraculous power to solve it. Nothing in the gospel for Easter warrants that assumption. It does not say how the stone was rolled away from the door of the sepulchre. It merely states that when the women looked they saw that the stone was rolled away. It may have been rolled away in a perfectly natural way, and probably was. For God works through normal processes rather than in spite of them.

Of course, it is altogether possible that God's ways of helping us are so prosaic that we do not recognize them as His ways. They are, nevertheless, a very present help in time of trouble; indeed, we could not get along without them for even a single day. What would we do without the measure of strength and skill and intelligence, which God gives us, together with the power to grow and develop physically, mentally and spiritually? And would it not be unfortunate, if He never provided us with moments of insight and incentive, of inspiration and encouragement, of happiness and satisfaction? Where would we be but for friends and neighbors and loved ones, who providentially stand by, together with a host of folk especially trained and qualified to give us aid and counsel? How fortunate we are that God put it into the hearts of men to establish agencies and institutions of serving love and helpful learning for our benefit! And think of the riches of His grace, so freely offered to us in the Word and the sacraments, and of the privilege we have to go to Him in prayer, assured that He will hear us! We cannot say that He does not afford us the help we need for the normal situations of life.

And withal God still provides us abundantly with all the necessaries of life. His good earth has not yet lost its ability to produce. Sunshine and rain, seed-time and harvest, have not ceased. In spite of our extravagance and wastefulness, the resources of nature are still ample to sustain us in abundance and peace. There is no evidence that God's love is waning, or that His grace is giving out. Each new day brings with it strength to carry our burdens and courage to fulfill our duties. There is no end to the resources God makes available to us. He provides ways and means enough and to spare for our usual needs. What right have we to demand further help of Him, until we have exhausted our present possibilities?

Moreover, are we not quite guilty of blasphemy, when we wantonly misuse or abuse God's provisions, and hold Him responsible for the precarious situations that result from our ignorance and folly, our envy and greed, our miserable mismanagement and merciless competition? Is He to blame for the horrible mess that is due to the selfishness and frailty of man and causes so many headaches and heartaches?

No, the trouble is that we give primacy to the material rather than to the spiritual things of life. We think we will be secure, if we have a fortune or fame, position or power. We seek money and might, influence and prestige, and put our trust in them. Nor are we any too scrupulous about the way we get them. We forget our Saviour's advice to seek first the kingdom of God and His righteousness, and His assurance that God knows the things we have need of and will provide us with them. We fail to keep in position of primacy those great, eternal, moral principles and values of which the kingdom of God is the symbol and realization. The kingdom of God is a kingdom of justice and truth, of equity and righteousness, of goodwill, human brotherhood and peace. These are the things that really count; these are the real values of life. If we have these, we can banish our fears, for they lead to freedom and democracy, to peace and harmony, to joy and happiness. No, "the fault is not in our stars, but in ourselves, that we are underlings."

We have no occasion to be anxious and apprehensive, if we live and act as the children of God, following the example and teachings of our Lord and Saviour. God is still our Father, and takes care of us. We are still His children, and brothers one of another. Let us, therefore, gratefully acknowledge the constant and abundant provision God makes for our welfare, and confidently meet our situations in an intelligently Christian way. If situations arise with which we cannot cope, let us leave them confidently in His hands. Experience has taught us that we are wise to do this, and as God's children we cannot do otherwise.

We know from experience how foolish we are, when we worry and do not trust Him. We have never yet prevented or changed a single situation by worrying about it; we have only made ourselves less able to cope with it. And we have discovered, time and again, that the disasters we dreaded failed to materialize, and the opportunities we thought were gone came back to us. For life has a way of developing along the most unexpected lines. "God moves in a mysterious way His wonders to perform." Unexpectedly something new comes into a situation before the fatal moment arrives, and everything turns out entirely different from what we anticipated. Even when we said, in anticipation of some great difficulty, "If I have got to go through with that, I'll die," we went through with it, and lived to tell it. We somehow find a way to go on living despite our difficulties, for there is a live-principle by which God enables us to do it.

In our saner moments we know there is a Living God, whom we can trust to take care of us and our loved ones, in life and in death. Today we rejoice and confidently exclaim, "I know that my Redeemer liveth." Instead of letting ourselves get into a pitiful state of self-distrust and fear, let us remember that "blessed is the man that maketh the Lord his trust." "God is our Refuge and Strength, a very present help in trouble: therefore will not we fear, though the earth be removed; and though the mountains be carried into the midst of the sea." "The eternal God is thy refuge, and underneath are the everlasting arms." "As the mountains are round about Jerusalem, so the Lord is round about his people." "As thy days so shall thy strength be."

The character and disposition of God warrant faith in Him. He is our Father, and "like as a father pitieth his children, so the Lord pitieth them that fear him." He has the attributes that enable Him to meet our situation, and He has promised not to leave us nor forsake us. In Him we have an object of faith, which, as Professor Whitehead has expressed it, "stands beyond, behind and within the passing flux of immediate things."

To be sure, there are things that are inevitable. In a recent article in the *Christian Century,* Gloria Harkness wrote: "There are conditions so unalterable that neither prayer nor human effort will avail to change them. Death comes to all. Its coming may be retarded but not forever, and the disease that is its precursor may have to be accepted as incurable. The limb cut off or the eye plucked out will not grow again. Our lost youth will not return. The economic resources once so readily available may be gone —gone not to be recovered in our lifetime. When the shadows thicken and our loved ones die, they will not come back in the loved familiar form. When the night of war comes upon the world, separations, sufferings, and the surrender of much that is precious in the old familiar ways must be accepted as inevitable."

If these things are inevitable, it is apparently futile to worry about them, and to anticipate them with fear and trembling. But, surely, they are not necessarily unfortunate because they are inescapable. There would have been no Easter had there been no Calvary. We must enter by faith and experience into the fellowship of Christ's sufferings, if we would become clothed with the power of His resurrection. Many a person has learned how "sweet are the uses of adversity." Abiding values come out of seeming misfortunes, and through the discipline of suffering we acquire them. And when we have them, we discover they are worth the price they cost.

To put it in the trenchant words of Dean Brown: "It may be suggested that no earthly father possessed by an honest affection for his children would suffer them to undergo such pain and distress as we can readily discover in this present world. But it is conceivable that all the struggles and trials to which humanity is here exposed may find their moral justification in a certain disciplinary and educative value as yet imperfectly understood. The entire world-process in certain aspects of its life 'groaneth and travaileth together in pain until now' waiting for something to declare its deeper meaning. 'Waiting for the manifestation of the sons of God!' Waiting for that higher type of human character, slowly wrought out ofttimes in agony and bloody sweat, to emerge and take control of the governable elements in that world process in the interest of the spiritual ends for which it was originally designed."

"In that event," he continues, "the high goal reached at last by the heirs of the promise would vindicate the purpose of the One who ordained the rough road to be traveled by those who would gain the supreme spiritual achievement. No movement, no process can be judged by the rude and lowly stable where it is born nor by the steep, hard way it may traverse in that period of discipline when obedience is learned by the things suffered. Let it be judged in every case by the throne which it is finally able to ascend!"

In the light of all this, the man who professes faith in God, and says, "I know that my Redeemer liveth," and yields to fear and worry notwithstanding, is either a hypocrite or a fool. His inconsistency can lead us to no other conclusion. If we believe in God, and know that our Redeemer liveth, we will trust God and not worry, do what we can in accordance with His will in situations that permit us to act, and confidently leave in His hands situations with which we cannot cope. As we do this, we will be enabled to say with ever increasing assurance, "I know that my Redeemer liveth."

Let me suggest, therefore, that, as we seek God's guidance in daily devotions, we use a prayer, which I recently discovered. I have been unable to establish the origin of it, but it reflects the conclusions of my discourse at this point. Listen to it closely. "O God, our heavenly Father, grant us the serenity of mind to accept that which cannot be changed; the courage to change that which can be changed, and the wisdom to know the one from the other; through Jesus Christ, Thy Son, our Lord. Amen."

I am afraid, however, that many of us today are facing situations in our private lives, our domestic relationships, our world, that will never be bettered, until we are changed ourselves. Not that I would imply that we can easily change ourselves. That would be sheer nonsense. For we cannot do it. We must be born again. That calls for more than a decision on our part to be different henceforth. It requires the power of the Holy Spirit. It demands the self-denial, self-sacrifice and self-surrender involved in following Christ.

What happens, when men become aware of the living presence of the Risen Christ and follow Him, is revealed in the sequence of events that took place, the first Easter day, after the women discovered that the stone was rolled away from the door of the sepulchre.

When the women saw that the stone was rolled away, they entered the sepulchre. "And entering the sepulchre, they saw a young man sitting at the right side, clothed in a long white garment." They were so frightened at the sight of him, that they failed to grasp immediately what he said to them. "They went out quickly and fled from the sepulchre; for they trembled and were amazed: neither said they any thing to any man: for they were afraid."

But, as they fled, the words which "the young man" had spoken to them kept resounding in their ears, until finally they stopped, breathlessly to ponder the meaning of them. They were wonderful words; reassuring from first to last, but quite unbelievable. For "the young man" had said: "Be not affrighted: Ye seek Jesus of Nazareth, which was crucified: he is risen; he is not here: behold the place where they laid him."

Then suddenly Mary Magdalene saw Jesus, for He appeared unto her first. Quick as a flash she hastened to where the disciples were gathered together, tearfully mourning the loss of the Lord, and told them He was alive. They would not believe it.

But presently He appeared unto them also—"appeared in another form unto two of them, as they walked, and went into the country"; "appeared unto the eleven as they sat at meat; and upraided them with their unbelief and hardness of heart because they believed not them which had seen him after he was risen"—until somehow His presence moved through that first Easter day with tremendous convincingness, and left none save Thomas to doubt that He was alive.

When Jesus had convinced the disciples that He had risen and was alive, He said unto them, "Go ye into all the world and preach the gospel to every creature." "And they went forth," the record says, "and preached everywhere, the Lord working with them, and confirming the word with signs following."

In other words, the disciples became aware of the living presence of the Risen Lord. They were convinced that their Redeemer was alive, and under the constraint of that conviction they went abroad and shared the secret of their salvation with people everywhere. Yet it was not a conviction which they reached readily. It was not created by evidence of an empty tomb. Nor was it dependent upon the nature of the resurrection body. It came by the process of personal experience. But that experience wrought a tremendous change in them.

They became entirely different men. They had been quite disappointed and disillusioned as a result of the crucifixion, death and burial of the Master. They had not been able to understand it. It had driven them to despair. They had lost all hope. "We had hoped that it was he who should redeem Israel," they had said. And, when it apparently was not He, they had decided that there was nothing left for them to do, but to take up life where they had left it, before they began to follow Him. Cowed and crushed in spirit, they were somewhere in Jerusalem, talking it all over, when the news of the Resurrection reached them.

But now they were not disheartened and despondent. They no longer disbelieved and despaired. They were confident and courageous in the knowledge of the Risen

Lord. Their inhibitions of fear dropped off them like broken chains, and they valiantly went forth, proclaiming the gospel of a Risen Lord and sealing it with their blood. In the power of the Resurrection they had the faith to do and dare and die for the Lord. And, when men sought the reason for the faith that was within them, they found it sufficing simply to say, "He showed himself alive."

They founded a fellowship of faith to which they admitted all who sought to be free from the bondage of sin and endowed with the glorious liberty wherewith Christ doth set men free. In that fellowship they called men to repentance and faith, and challenged them to live at their best, if haply they might attain unto the perfection which we know and have in Christ Jesus, and glorify God thereby. That fellowship has grown and developed, until today it encircles the entire globe. It finds expression in the work and worship of the whole Christian Church on earth, and touches the common life with a redemptive power that can be matched in no other institution in the world.

If it be true, that all great movements are but the lengthened shadows of great men, then this truth finds expression as nowhere else in the corporate life of the Christian Church. For the disciples became great through the power of the Risen Lord, and the genius of the Church is rooted and grounded in their conviction that Christ Jesus triumphed over sin and death and the power of the devil, when He came striding down the garden of Joseph of Arimathaea, the first Easter day, and showed Himself to them alive. Constrained by that conviction, Christians the world over crowd their churches to the doors this day, and, amid much pomp and circumstance, lift their hearts and voices high to sing their great Redeemer's praise.

In the face of all this, we can clearly see what happens, when a man becomes aware of the living presence of the Risen Lord, and follows Him. It makes a profound difference in him. He becomes quite a new man. He acquires those sterling qualities that combine to constitute the noblest type of human character. He approximates, if he does not completely achieve, the perfection which is Christ's. He also finds something in Christ that challenges him to launch out, in a spirit of reckless self-abandon, upon the sea of adventurous service, for the glory of God and the good of humanity. He finds the courage to face the most hazardous situations without flinching. Nor is this surprising. For upon the high level of fellowship with Christ, communing means partaking, and we kindle to the same spirit that dwells in Him.

If, therefore, we are truly His disciples, we will bear the unmistakable marks of men who have been in contact with the Risen Lord. If we can honestly say from experience, "I know that my Redeemer liveth," we will produce the evidence to prove it, for the world will be convinced of the reality of our spiritual experience only if our lives burn and shine with the light divine. Moreover, we will tell others the source of our salvation, so that they, too, may become partakers of the unsearchable riches in Christ Jesus. We will spread the good news of salvation unto the uttermost parts of the earth, in the hope that the kingdom of God may come and His will be done on earth as it is in heaven.

But we will be careful not to give people any wrong impressions about Christ Jesus, lest they entertain false expectations and come to grief. We will remember the sad plight that befell the disciples, when Jesus was crucified, dead and buried. For they followed Him under a mistaken impression. They thought that He was the one anointed of God to fulfill the Messianic hope which the Jews cherished.

This hope was based upon the assumption that, with the coming of the Messiah, providentially the enemies of the Jewish people would be destroyed, the nations of the earth would be subjugated to the Jews, and a new world-empire would be established, with Jerusalem as its capital and Messiah as its king. The law would go forth out of Zion; men would beat their swords into ploughshares and their spears into pruninghooks; nation would not rise up against nation, neither would they learn war any more. Peace on earth, good will toward men would ensue, and the Jews would enjoy everlasting happiness. It was a hope quite visionary in character, and it was quite incapable of fulfillment by our Lord, for it was conceived in bitterness and rancor and born of envy, hatred and revenge. But, even so, it was the Jews' hope of redemption, and their idea of the coming of the kingdom of God. Nor dare we deride it, for even in our day there are nations at war, putting their trust in their leaders as in a Messiah and expecting victory with results no less fantastic than those the Jews expected.

While Jesus said and did nothing to encourage their expectation, but rather discouraged it and foretold the tragic issue of His ministry, the disciples persisted in clinging to it. They began to look for its fulfillment, the moment Jesus began to set His face steadfastly toward Jerusalem. When He staged His triumphal entry into the city, they concluded that the decisive moment had come. One word from Him and heaven-sent armies would arrive, rout the Romans from the land, set Jerusalem free and enthrone Him as king.

But, much to their sorrow and disappointment, Jesus did not leap to the pinnacle of the temple, rend the clouds of heaven asunder, summon a vast army of angels and archangels, expel the Romans from power and force them to fall prostrate at His feet and acknowledge Him to be king. For He did not conceive this to be His mission. He wept over the city, as He came within sight of it, and prophesied its impending destruction. When He reached the temple, He "looked round upon all things," and then quietly returned to Bethany, from whence He had come.

No wonder the disciples were dismayed, when the Roman soldiers nailed Jesus to the cross. No wonder they despaired, when He was taken down dead from the cross. No wonder they buried all their hopes with Him, when He was laid to rest in the tomb in "Joseph's lovely garden." They paid the price of placing their trust in hopes founded upon illusions.

Jesus was, indeed, the Messiah, the one anointed of God, to bring redemption. But His redemptive ministry was not meant to be confined to the people of Israel. Nor was it intended simply for their political restoration. Neither was it to be accomplished by the use of celestial armies and magically made empires, the employment of hatreds and exploitation and revenge, the promise of eternal bliss in any bourgeois sense of the term. It was a ministry conceived by God in love, and dedicated to the proposition that all men should be free from sin and death to enjoy everlasting life. It was designed to be restricted by no boundaries, no seas, no landmarks; to extend to all sorts and conditions of men, regardless of color, caste or clime, and to include every conceivable want in the whole catalogue of human infirmity and need.

To express it more precisely, Christ Jesus came to reconcile the world to God. His ministry of reconciliation was based upon certain fundamental principles, which can be stated very simply. God is our Father, and we are His children. By virtue of this fact, we are brothers one of another. For the proper expression and maintenance of these relationships, love is essential. True love expresses itself in perfect obedience to the will of God. Anything short of such obedience is sin. Sin separates a man from God, and apart from God there is no life. There is, therefore, no death save the separation from God which results from sin. "He that doeth the will of God abideth forever." If we love God, and prove it by a life of perfect obedience to His will, we are assured of eternal life.

No man may claim to love God, however, who does not love his brother also. Love to God must evince itself in love to one's fellows. To be free from sin, therefore, and to escape the door of death, both here and hereafter, we must be in right relationship to God and to our fellow men. The plight of men individually and collectively will be improved only as we come to this knowledge and act upon it. For ultimately all our ills are attributable to sin. And there is not one of us who does not sin. Whether our failure to do God's will is an act of omission or commission, done deliberately or in ignorance, consciously or unconsciously, it is, nevertheless, responsible for our troubles, when, where and howsoever they may befall us. Our only salvation lies in redemption from sin.

We may obtain such redemption through Christ Jesus. He came to save men from sin, and to bring them into conformity with the mind and will of God. To this end, He called men to repentance and faith in God, and commanded them to obey His twofold law of love, which embraces the essential teachings of the law and the prophets. He was Himself obedient unto death, even the death of the cross. That is why He rose from the dead, and lives and reigns to all eternity. If we would obtain redemption, and have everlasting life, we must emulate Him in this respect. To be able to do so, however, we must acquire His nature.

Some of us may claim to possess His nature. We may be able to substantiate our claim with evidence that "the old Adam in us" is "drowned and destroyed by daily sorrow and repentance, together with all sins and evil lusts," and that "the new man" daily comes forth and rises to "live in the presence of God in righteousness and purity for ever." Well and good! But not until all men are "born again" and "walk in the newness of life," will justice and truth, equity and righteousness, peace, goodwill and human brotherhood be universally evident as tokens of the realization of the kingdom of God and of the reign of love.

Every day that we put off the decision to follow Christ, we forfeit the benefits of life, and prevent the kingdom of God from coming to us. Unless we seek salvation now, we may never obtain it; for, at any time, the day may come, and catch us unawares, when an accounting will be demanded of us to see what disposition we have made of the opportunity afforded us in Christ to be reconciled to God. Then it may be too late.

While these principles are not the unabridged version of "the old, old story of Jesus and His love," they suffice to show us the contrast of the hope of the Jews, and point out what the disciples should have expected, had they understood the purpose of the Master.

Unless people understand the message and mission of Jesus, they run the risk of being sadly disappointed, when they follow Him. Many are at this very moment in the mood in which the disciples were, just before the Resurrection of our Lord. It is a mood as unwarranted as that of the women, who vainly wondered who would roll them away the stone from the door of the sepulchre, and it is just as futile. For Christ is our witness that "they that trust in the Lord" and do His will triumph in the end. It is a mood, moreover, that can be attributed to any one of many causes; but it inevitably comes, when men pin their faith to hopes that rest upon illusions.

For this reason, we must do all we can to dispel the illusions about Christ. It is heartrending to see a man broken in spirit, with faith in God and man gone, and none in himself, because he had high expectations, and lived in joyful and hopeful anticipation of their fulfillment, only to be rudely awakened one day to the realization that they were in vain. I do not understand the person who deliberately prefers death to life, and I pity the one who is dead and does not know it. For the man is not dead whose soul has been freed from the limitations of the flesh and abides with God. The man is dead who lives apart from God. But I deplore the plight of the man who chooses to follow Christ, and fails to find his dreams come true in Him, because he follows Him under some false impression. There is, incidentally, a vast difference between the man who follows Christ under false impressions and the one who follows Him under false pretenses.

Let us, therefore, set ourselves and others straight about Christ. If there be those, who think they can follow Him with divided allegiance or with preconceived plans and prospects for the welfare of the world and of themselves, let us disillusion them. We must "renounce the devil, and all his works, and all his ways," deny ourselves completely and commit ourselves, body, soul and spirit to Christ, if we would be His followers. That spells undivided loyalty; calls for unbroken faith and fealty. It implies forgetting our nicely conceived notions about what ails the world, and how it can be cured, and accepting His prognosis and prescription.

If there be those, who despair of the coming of the kingdom of God in our time; or others, who expect it to come in a sensational and spectacular manner, and establish itself by a sudden miraculous transformation of the present order of things; or still others, who picture it to be like the earthly kingdoms we know; let us not deride them or despise them. They are earnest and devout people, in spite of their misgivings and mistaken ideas. They are in need of enlightenment. They must be reminded that Jesus regarded this world as God's world, and His kingdom as in the process of coming and, indeed, even already present in germ. For the kingdom of God is "that society of redeemed personalities, of which Christ is at once the ideal and the mediator, the union of whose members, one with another and with God in the community of holy love, progressively in history, constitutes the end for which the world exists." Jesus expressly told the Pharisees, in response to their question when the kingdom of God should come, "The kingdom of God cometh not with observation, neither shall they say, 'Lo here! or, Lo there!' for lo, the kingdom of God is (already) in the midst of you." And we believe that the second petition of our Lord's Prayer is answered, "when our heavenly Father gives us His Holy Spirit, so that by His grace we believe His holy Word, and live a godly life here on earth, and in heaven forever."

If there be those, who would capture the kingdom of heaven by violence, let us discourage them, and urge them to substitute the power of love for the love of power. For, if love is the end they desire, love must be the means they employ. Love begets love. Peace on earth, goodwill toward men, will never be realized by destroying or forcibly restraining all those who do not love. "Not by might nor by power, but by my spirit, saith the Lord of hosts."

If there be people anywhere, with wrong impressions of any kind, touching the place and purpose of Christ Jesus, let us set them straight. Above all, let us be sure that we are straight ourselves. Let there be no illusions! Then we will find our hopes in Christ fulfilled, and He will not be disappointed in us. We will reflect His character in every situation that confronts us in life, and enjoy the happiness that comes and abides with those who dedicate themselves to the avowed purpose of living in right relationship to God and to their fellow men, to the glory of God, who redeemed us in Christ Jesus, the Saviour of men.